# DIFFERENTIATED INSTRUCTION

## Meeting the Educational Needs of All Students in Your Classroom

### Marcie Nordlund

ScarecrowEducation
Lanham, Maryland • Toronto • Oxford
2003

*KH*

A SCARECROWEDUCATION BOOK

Published in the United States of America
by ScarecrowEducation
An imprint of The Rowman & Littlefield Publishing Group, Inc.
4501 Forbes Boulevard, Suite 200, Lanham, Maryland 20706
www.scaroweducation.com

PO Box 317
Oxford
OX2 9RU, UK

British Library Cataloguing in Publication Information Available

**Library of Congress Cataloging-in-Publication Data**
Nordlund, Marcie, 1953–
    Differentiated instruction : meeting the educational needs of all students
in your classroom / Marcie Nordlund.
        p.  cm.
    "A ScarecrowEducation book."
    Includes bibliographical references and index.
    ISBN 0-8108-4702-7 (pbk. : alk. paper)
        1. Individualized instruction.  2. Mixed ability grouping in education.
    I. Title.

LB1031 .N64 2003
371.39'4—dc21

                                                    2002044667


⊗™ The paper used in this publication meets the minimum requirements of
American National Standard for Information Sciences—Permanence of Paper
for Printed Library Materials, ANSI/NISO Z39.48-1992.
Manufactured in the United States of America.

10/25/04

# CONTENTS

| | | |
|---|---|---:|
| **1** | The Big Picture | 1 |
| **2** | How to Get Started | 7 |
| **3** | Students with Cognitive Impairments | 21 |
| **4** | Children with Difficulties Attending to Task | 29 |
| **5** | Students with Learning Disabilities and Students Identified as Slow Learners | 37 |
| **6** | Children Whose Native Language Is Not English | 49 |
| **7** | Children with Above-Average Abilities | 59 |
| **8** | Students at Risk of School Failure | 67 |
| **9** | Classroom Management | 73 |
| **10** | Bringing the Staff Together | 87 |
| Rules | | 99 |
| Bibliography | | 101 |
| Index | | 105 |
| About the Author | | 107 |

# ❶

# THE BIG PICTURE

In 1986, Madeleine Will, the assistant secretary of the Office of Special Education, wrote a paper entitled *Educating Students with Learning Problems: A Shared Responsibility.* This manuscript signaled the beginning of the movement to educate students with diverse learning needs together in the same classroom. The concept included educating students with mild to moderate special learning needs within the regular classroom. In more recent years, this idea has expanded to include a wide spectrum of learning abilities, styles, and needs, including students who demonstrate above-average intelligence, students who are considered "at risk" of school failure, students with cultural/language differences, students who are educationally disadvantaged, students who have a slow learning rate, and students who qualify for special education services (Choate 1993). In addition, such factors as race, ethnicity, socioeconomic status, educational history, family values, primary language, and gender can also affect a child's education. All of this is occurring at a time when test scores are being monitored more closely than ever and school finances are tighter than ever. Teachers are clearly challenged by the task of diversifying instruction in order to help every child meet full potential.

Federal and state governments offer funding to help certain groups of challenged learners. Money is available through what are called "Title" programs to hire additional staff for low-income students. Specific funding is granted to schools for students for whom English is a second language. Additional monies are offered for special education students. And yet what happens to the student who has not been classified in any of these categories but needs additional assistance and modifications in order to meet her full potential? Who is responsible for educating these students? The Title I or special education teacher may consider the attention deficit student not part of the bilingual program. The bilingual teacher may not feel responsible for the at-risk student. And no one may be anxious to work with the homeless, transient, or difficult-to-motivate student. How far do we pass the buck in educating these challenged learners?

We must consider education as an array of services. Every teacher, whether specially trained in special education, reading, or English as a second language, as well as those trained primarily in standard education, must assume responsibility for educating all students. Students need to be educated wherever is most appropriate and by whomever is best suited to meet the child's learning needs. Special education students are no longer educated in the small room hidden behind the boiler. A resource teacher working with a group of special education students on a phonics lesson can often include a child who is not classified yet who needs additional assistance that is offered in a group made up primarily of identified special education students with Individual Educational Plans (IEPs). Title reading instruction is often taught by use of a "push-in" model of services—having the Title teacher work with identified students in their regular classroom along with many students who need assistance. (See chapter 5 for a more expanded discussion of push-in services.) At the same time, many children in a classroom may need modifications made by the classroom teacher, either on a temporary or a long-term basis. These modifications and curricular expectations must be fluid for each child, based on the content of the lesson and the learning ability of each student.

There are three methods of differentiating instruction for any curricular area: modifying the content, the process of learning, and the end product (Tomlinson 2001). When modifying the content of a lesson, a teacher must decide the core concepts that every child must master. It is very difficult to limit a teacher to only a handful of concepts for each unit that is to be mastered by every student. However, once this core content is established, then the complexity can be adjusted as needed. When modifying the instructional process, the teacher is able to vary the activities and strategies utilized to teach each concept. A more challenged learner would require more direct instruction while a more capable student would be able to engage in more independent learning. Finally, by changing the depth, amount, or independence of products either in the form of tests, projects, written work, or oral presentations, teachers are able to make lessons meaningful and applicable for every student. Table 1.1 shows the framework for differentiating between the content, process, and product.

Whenever modifying any of these areas, teachers should first determine the expectations of instruction for average students. If the chart is to be completed for a research project, the average student might need to examine all aspects of the topics for the Content component. The process for teaching the average student might include modeling by the teacher, direct instruction, and time for independent work. The final product may be a five-page paper. This same assignment would be more meaningful for a gifted student if the content expectations were to study the topic more thoroughly, understanding the effects, relationships, or causes in greater depth. The process of instruction

**Table 1.1.   Three Ways to Differentiate Instruction**

|  | Challenged | Average | Gifted |
|---|---|---|---|
| CONTENT |  |  |  |
| What |  |  |  |
| PROCESS |  |  |  |
| How |  |  |  |
| PRODUCT |  |  |  |
| Evaluation |  |  |  |

would include more independent study, with less direct instruction by the teacher. The final product might include computer graphics or Internet research. A student with learning challenges may only be expected to research three areas of the topic. The teacher, either classroom or support teacher, would use more direct instruction and repetition. The final product may be a one-page paper or a group project, as demonstrated in table 1.2.

---

Rule #1
Always remember the purpose of instruction.

---

If the purpose of a unit is to teach the students how to complete a research paper, then the process is more important than the content or the product. These same students in future years may need more concentration on a more sophisticated product with greater emphasis on the content. By determining the purpose of instruction, the core concepts can be established and prioritized. The focus of the content, process, and product can be adjusted throughout a unit of instruction, throughout a grade level, or throughout a child's education.

**Table 1.2.    Three Ways to Differentiate Instruction**

|  | Challenged | Average | Gifted |
|---|---|---|---|
| CONTENT | Three crucial points Key concepts | All aspects of the topic | In-depth study |
| What |  |  |  |
| PROCESS | Direct instruction of each step in the research process | Modeling Independent work Review and practice | Minimal instruction with probing questions for independent study |
| How |  |  |  |
| PRODUCT | Group paper of one page | Five-page paper | PowerPoint presentation with computer-generated graphs and tables |
| Evaluation |  |  |  |

In general, several guidelines need to be followed in order to create an effective classroom of diverse learning:

1. The classroom teacher and the educational team, made up of support staff and administrators, must view diversified learning as a positive experience for students.
2. The classroom teacher and the educational team must believe that students from a variety of educational, cultural, and socioeconomic backgrounds enhance the learning climate for all students.
3. An atmosphere of cooperation (and not competition) must be established for both students and staff.
4. Teachers must utilize all available resources to support learning activities. This requires individualizing learning for each student by arranging the classroom and the entire school for small-group, large-group, and independent learning. A fluid building is developed, students are able to utilize the entire school as their classroom, and teachers can promote student movement throughout the school as determined by learning needs and curriculum considerations.

**2**

# HOW TO GET STARTED

The idea of differentiating instruction for all children within a classroom can seem overwhelming. This is especially true for first-year teachers who do not have a solid understanding of the curriculum. When beginning a career in education or when changing grade levels or subjects, the most important task is to thoroughly learn the curriculum and state standards for the subject area. That is quite a task! Therefore, most of the methods discussed in this book are not recommended until a teacher has taught a grade level for at least one year. However, one method of differentiating instruction can be used immediately: the idea of categorizing levels of abstraction during instruction using Bloom's Taxonomy.

## BLOOM'S TAXONOMY

One of the concepts learned in undergraduate work in education is one of the most important tools for diversifying instruction. In 1956, Benjamin Bloom developed a system of categorizing levels of abstractions of questions (Bloom 1956). This taxonomy utilized different levels of instruction based on a person's cognitive ability. In table 2.1, the hierarchy

Table 2.1.  Using Bloom's Taxonomy

| Level | Definition | Questions |
|---|---|---|
| **Knowledge** | Recall<br>Regurgitation of facts | Tell<br>List<br>Memorize<br>Give the definition |
| **Comprehension** | Repeat in own words | Give an example<br>Explain<br>Retell |
| **Application** | Apply to a new situation | Build<br>Demonstrate<br>Make<br>Develop |
| **Analysis** | Study parts | Compare<br>Analyze<br>Categorize<br>Contrast |
| **Evaluation** | Give opinion backed by facts | Evaluate<br>Judge<br>Critique |
| **Synthesis** | Create a new concept from<br>learned material | Design<br>Create<br>Construct<br>Develop |

of Bloom's Taxonomy is shown. Key words that can be used to pose questions at different levels of ability are also shown.

These levels are given in a hierarchy ranging from the easiest to the most difficult. One of the easiest ways to begin diversifying instruction is to apply this theory to class discussions. Students with mild cognitive impairments or students who are slow learners will do best if given opportunities to answer questions at the knowledge or comprehension level. These should be the first questions asked by the teacher to enhance the self-confidence of challenged learners. Often, when challenged learners hear questions they don't understand, these students will "turn off" to learning immediately. If they are asked questions they are able to answer, they will continue to remain on task and engaged in the class discussion. However, higher-level thinking questions must also be included in class discussions in order to inspire all students. Because many students with learning disabilities have at least average intelligence and learn differently than do their peers, these students often do best when given opportunities to demonstrate their understanding of a concept by utilizing questions requiring synthesis or evaluation. These students require direct instruction in the construction of their answers but are able to think at this higher level. Students with learning disabilities need to be taught step by step how to answer a question at this level of understanding. For example, they must be taught the difference between "compare" and "contrast." Without direct instruction, students with learning disabilities will answer that they don't know the answer to the question, when in reality they don't understand the question itself.

Table 2.2 can be used by teachers as a framework for using Bloom's Taxonomy to differentiate questions during classroom discussion. This strategy can also be used when writing test questions. Questions at the lower end of the taxonomy would demonstrate that students with learning challenges have mastered the core concepts of instruction while questions from the higher end would be used to stimulate higher level thinking in more gifted learners.

An example of a class discussion of a history lesson regarding the lives of early American settlers is shown in table 2.3. While the information covered in each question is similar, the level of understanding needed to

**Table 2.2.   Putting Bloom's Taxonomy to Work**
Write a question for each level in Bloom's Taxonomy

**Knowledge**

---

**Comprehension**

---

**Application**

---

**Analysis**

---

**Evaluation**

---

**Synthesis**

---

**Table 2.3.   Putting Bloom's Taxonomy to Work (Completed)**
Tools Developed by the Early Settlers

| | |
|---|---|
| **Knowledge** | Name two tools developed by early settlers. |
| **Comprehension** | Give an example of a tool used today that has its basis in early settler times. |
| **Application** | Using only paper-towel tubes, build a model of any tool developed by early settlers. |
| **Analysis** | Compare/contrast the nonmotorized tools of today and the farm tools used by early settlers. |
| **Evaluation** | What tool developed by early settlers had the greatest impact on our lives today? Why? |
| **Synthesis** | What tools do we use today that you think will be modified for the future? How? |

answer each question varies significantly. Questions at the knowledge and comprehension levels are used to check literal comprehension, while evaluation and synthesis questions delve to a deeper level of understanding.

As with any new method, this may appear bulky at first; with practice, however, teachers automatically begin phrasing their questions, either on tests or during class discussions, with this theory in mind. By varying the level of questions throughout instruction, students can either be reinforced for their efforts or challenged into their highest level of thinking.

## CURRICULUM-BASED INSTRUCTION

Curriculum-based instruction is a method of using the course content and daily lessons as a determination of a student's instructional needs. In this strategy, the teacher assesses the child's current skills in the content and assesses these skills frequently to determine daily progress. The classroom teacher must determine the most important skills while the team, generally made up of the classroom teacher, special educator, reading teacher, and principal, determines which of these core skills the student can master. This assessment process helps to establish the content, process, and product expected from each student as previously discussed.

Specifically, the first step in developing curriculum-based instruction is to analyze the skills determined to be required for the lesson. For example, if the lesson at hand is to write a three-paragraph essay, the skill breakdown might include the ability to sequence thoughts, write in full sentences, and use punctuation and capitalization. If the student is significantly lacking in any of these prerequisite skills, then direct instruction must take place to teach these skills. Much of education is a hierarchy of learning. If the child does not possess the skills at the bottom of the hierarchy, then instruction must begin at this level. Once a skill breakdown has been completed and the requirements for the typical student established, curriculum expansion can take place. The teacher can then decide appropriate instruction for the child with greater-than-average abilities. In the above example, the gifted child may be asked to use more descriptors, expand the average sentence length, or consider more details when writing. It is important to note that the child with above-average abilities should not be required to simply do more, but instead should be challenged by going deeper into the topic (see chapter 7). The next level in this hierarchy of instruction would be to use the same objective, but an alternative method. As learned in chapter 1, it is important to remember the purpose of instruction. If the purpose of writing a three-paragraph essay is to teach how to organize and sequence thoughts, how to stay on a topic, and how to develop a topic, then it is unimportant whether the student with learning challenges writes the essay in longhand or utilizes a computer to help get the thoughts down logically. Some students may need the assistance of a spell-check system. For others, extended time or an opportunity to work in a quiet room may benefit instruction. None of these accommodations would interfere with the integrity of the assignment.

Some students may need more modifications. For the student with more learning challenges, using the same objective (writing an essay) with reduced complexity may be more appropriate. This student may need to work on some of the prerequisite skills such as punctuation or staying on topic before attempting to write a three-paragraph essay. It is more beneficial to have a student successfully complete a well-written one-paragraph essay than to be frustrated and attempt to write a poorly constructed three-paragraph essay.

---

Rule #2
Always begin with success.

---

If we let a child begin instruction where he feels successful, this child will be willing to take more risks as learning becomes more motivational and successful. This rule is particularly true of children who are educationally disadvantaged, transient, or previously unsuccessful in their school experiences. These challenged learners have faced repeated failure in their academic careers and are fearful of taking risks educationally. Often, they feel it is better not to try than to look bad and fail.

When further modifications are necessary, the teacher may decide to stress only the main concept of instruction. If the purpose of instruction is to develop more details in writing, then a student at this level might only list descriptors or write a complete sentence. Sometimes, it is even necessary to use a lower grade-level curriculum for materials and strategies. One method to assist in this process is to leave plastic bins in the school copy area. As teachers copy worksheets for a specific grade level in a subject, they deposit one copy in the bin. Support staff or teachers in other grades are able to "pick and choose" to develop individualized packets of instruction for students who need these skills. When placed in a folder or cover, these worksheets can discreetly be used during seatwork times or for specialized instruction. However the individual educational needs of a student are met, it is imperative that a student's dignity be maintained. Although the student may require prerequisite skills that are taught in a lower grade level, it is important that other students not be aware that the child is doing lower grade-level work.

Continuing down the hierarchy of this chart, students with more significant learning challenges may have a totally different objective for a task. This is particularly true for special education students with Individual Educational Plans (IEPs). While the class is writing an essay, a child with special needs might be practicing writing her name, copying spelling words, or completing a job application. Although the goal of instruction is very different, the student may be learning a tremendous amount by watching the other students as role models. It is difficult to teach students with significant learning and behavioral challenges proper social skills or skills for completing tasks independently unless they are associating with their peers as they complete these tasks. Although the instruction and goals of these children are very different from those of the typical learner, these children are still accomplishing important goals.

The most major modification made to the standard curriculum is when the child necessitates a parallel curriculum. At times, the standard curriculum is nonmeaningful for a child with significant learning needs. It is then important for the child to engage in activities that will meet IEP goals. A functional curriculum (see chapter 3), a school job, an outdoor activity, cooking, or counting money may be important assets in a child's learning plan. This method of curriculum expansion can also be used with students with more mild learning challenges but in acute crisis. A child with extreme family problems may be unable to concentrate throughout an entire morning of instruction. This child might benefit from frequent breaks that involve brief physical movement in place of a parallel curriculum. A hyperactive child might find more success if given opportunities for physical exertion throughout the day. This might include tasks such as delivering milk to the kindergarten class, carrying PE equipment outside, or loading the pop machine in the teachers' lunchroom. Table 2.4 shows how one lesson can be used with modifications to teach students with above-average abilities through students with significant disabilities. This level of differentiation requires a very solid understanding of the curriculum as well as the educational needs of students who are gifted as well as students with learning challenges. This is

**Table 2.4. Differentiated Levels of Instruction**

| | |
|---|---|
| Skill Breakdown | (List all the skills necessary to complete the lesson accurately) |
| More Complex | (What gifted students should do) |
| Same Objective/Same Complexity | (Average learner) |
| Same Objective/Alternative Method | (Average cognitive ability student with special needs) |
| Main Concept | (Student with learning challenges) |
| Lower Grade Level | (Student with significant learning challenges) |
| Different Objective | (Student with cognitive impairment or autism) |
| Parallel Curriculum | (Student with cognitive impairment or autism) |

the most complex method of differentiation and should not be attempted by a first-year teacher.

## DETERMINING ESSENTIAL CONCEPTS

Once a teacher has a firm understanding of the curriculum and state standards, the teacher is able to begin modifying the curriculum to meet the educational needs of each student. This task is generally appropriate for a teacher in at least his second year of teaching. At that time, the classroom teacher is able to determine the most important parts of the curriculum (the core concepts) that every student must master. Although, as teachers, we would all like to believe that we can teach any child the entire curriculum, it is more realistic to understand that some children are more successful when presented with the most important material to learn. Just as a computer disk can become full of files, a child's mind can become full of concepts. It is the responsibility of the team to determine which important concepts should take up space on the child's "disk" because when the disk becomes full, it cannot take in any more information for storage.

---

Rule #3
The classroom teacher is the expert in
curriculum; the special education teacher
is the expert in special methods.

---

Because the classroom teacher intimately knows the curriculum for her grade level, that teacher is best able to determine the most important skills of each grade level/class. These core concepts should be determined at the district level when district curriculum guides are written. If a core-concept curriculum has not been written at the district level, then the classroom teacher must determine the most important concepts of instruction. One way these concepts can be determined is by having the classroom teacher complete the form seen in table 2.5 at the completion of each unit of study. At the beginning of the school year, the teacher should make many copies of this form. At the completion of

**Table 2.5.   Unit Focus**

Concepts
Vocabulary
Activities/Projects
Skills for Future Units of Instruction

each unit in any subject, the teacher can quickly fill out this form while the unit of study is readily available. Key concepts for each unit are determined by asking these questions:

- Is the concept used throughout a unit of study?
- Will the concept be used in other grades?
- Is the concept one that needs to be learned in an academic hierarchy?

If yes can be answered to any of these questions, then it is important to include these concepts. Although we'd like to think that every concept we teach is important, at times we must choose the most important concepts for mastery by more challenged learners.

The next step is to determine how to expand instruction on each of these units. After determining the key issues, the teacher can determine how to expand the curriculum so that every child may benefit from instruction. In table 2.6, the purpose of instruction for a specific unit is determined as well as the main concepts that every student should master. Gifted students are then considered with expansion projects to meet their needs, thus enabling the student to study the unit in greater depth. The teacher determines what modifications are necessary for challenged learners and what activities are not appropriate for significantly challenged learners (inclusion students). A completed example is seen in table 2.7. In this example, a third-grade teacher was teaching the fundamentals of an ecosystem. The teacher first needed to determine the four core concepts, the most important aspects of the curriculum that would be stressed to all students. Once the focus of instruction is determined, the teacher is able to strategize how to expand the curriculum to meet the needs of the gifted students. Additionally, modifications can be determined for both the moderately challenged learner and a child with significant learning challenges. Certain activities would be appropriate for all learners, while higher-level activities may not be

**Table 2.6.    Unit Curriculum Expansion**

| Purpose of Instruction: |
| --- |

| Four Main Concepts: |
| --- |

Concept #1:
Concept #2:
Concept #3:
Concept #4:

| Expansion for Gifted Students: |
| --- |

| Modifications for Challenged Learners: |
| --- |

| Activities Appropriate for Inclusion: |
| --- |

| Activities Inappropriate for Inclusion: |
| --- |

| Assistance Needed from Support Staff: |
| --- |

| Other Considerations: |
| --- |

relevant for students with significant learning challenges. An important consideration is the determination of specific activities that would require additional assistance from support staff. Determining which activities require assistance from support staff enables the teacher and the support staff member to plan more effectively.

Students are assessed to check their understanding of the material presented. Many methods of alternate assessment can be used when differentiating instruction.

Rule #4
Always remember the purpose of assessment.

**Table 2.7.   Unit Curriculum Expansion (Completed)**

**Purpose of Instruction:**

Students will demonstrate an understanding of the interdependency between living and nonliving things within an ecosystem.

**Four Main Concepts:**

**Concept #1:**  What is an ecosystem?
**Concept #2:**  What is a food chain?
**Concept #3:**  What are the living and nonliving elements within an ecosystem?
**Concept #4:**  How does an ecosystem stay in balance?

**Expansion for Gifted Students:**

PowerPoint presentation of an ecosystem
Effects of pollution on an ecosystem
Design a new ecosystem

**Modifications for Challenged Learners:**

Acting out steps of the food chain
Drawing pictures of living and nonliving elements

**Activities Appropriate for Inclusion:**

Dioramas and posters that include the different living and nonliving elements

**Activities Inappropriate for Inclusion:**

Research project

**Assistance Needed from Support Staff:**

Research project and computer assistance

**Other Considerations:**

When a student has learning challenges, it is not always appropriate to use standard testing methods to accurately determine how well the student has mastered the material. On the other hand, modifying assessment should never interfere with the integrity of the testing. By considering the purpose of assessment, a teacher can change the testing device while maintaining integrity. If the purpose of testing is to determine a child's reading level, then obviously the test cannot be read to the student. However, if the purpose of testing is to determine how well the student understands the key concepts of the Civil Rights movement, and the child has reading challenges, then having a proctor read the test to the student would ensure that the full scope of the student's understanding is adequately assessed. The child's reading problems would not interfere with the child's ability to relate learned knowledge. Other methods of alternate assessment include:

- Verbal tests
- Shortened tests
- Literal levels of questions
- More frequent tests
- Extended time for test completion
- Scribe (having another person write) for written responses
- Quiet place for testing
- IEP goal achievement as basis for grading
- Course project rather than written test
- Development of instructional packet with a variety of activities demonstrating knowledge.

It is more difficult for support staff to assist the classroom teacher and work with special learners in a differentiated classroom than in the old "pull-out" model. In the older model, support staff was assigned a certain number of minutes each week to work with individual students or small groups in a room other than the classroom. Little consideration was given to the curriculum within the classroom. Support staff schedules were relatively solid and easy to follow. In a differentiated classroom, support staff members base their services on when and how a student needs assistance with a particular part of the standard curriculum. IEP goals, LEP (Limited English Proficiency) goals, and Title (federal funding) goals are all written based on the state standards applied to all students. By having the classroom teacher determine in advance what specific projects or activities will require additional assistance from the support staff, support staff members are able to better plan their time. Support staff can collaborate to determine who will be responsible for assisting which students with which project. After completing the Unit Curriculum Expansion in table 2.7, teachers can determine which major project will necessitate assistance from support staff. The Yearly Project Plan seen in table 2.8 can then be used to help staff arrange schedules in advance of key projects.

Using this plan, classroom teachers first list when they would optimally like to schedule large projects or activities for their classroom. By filling out this chart, teachers can check to make sure they don't have

**Table 2.8.   Yearly Project Plan**

|  | English | Math | Social Studies | Science | Writing |
|---|---|---|---|---|---|
| September |  |  |  |  |  |
| October |  |  |  |  |  |
| November |  |  |  |  |  |
| December |  |  |  |  |  |
| January |  |  |  |  |  |
| February |  |  |  |  |  |
| March |  |  |  |  |  |
| April |  |  |  |  |  |
| May |  |  |  |  |  |

several large projects assigned simultaneously, especially for younger students. A faculty meeting is then scheduled, with each classroom teacher bringing this information. Large butcher-block paper is posted on the wall with a blank Project Plan chart. Each teacher fills in his optimal plan (with pencil). Each project/activity for each grade level is assigned a support person to assist (Title, special education, ESL, gifted, librarian, technology teacher). If too many large assignments are given at the same time, teachers must then negotiate with each other so that children receive the support they need. Not only does this system help student achievement, it goes a long way to build staff morale. Teachers are assured that they will have the needed help from support staff during major projects. Of course, changes in scheduling are expected during the school year, but both classroom teachers and support staff have a better idea of what to expect each month. If an activity does not require assistance from a support staff member, then the Yearly Project Plan can be completed without regards to support staff availability.

All of this planning does not occur overnight. Perhaps the most important rule of diversifying instruction is:

> Rule #5
> Use baby steps.

Many good ideas in education fail because educators have a tendency to quickly adopt new strategies without taking enough time to feel comfortable with the new concept. Any teacher beginning diversified instruction must first start by determining key concepts of instruction. Obviously, a first-year teacher or a teacher new to a grade level is unable to complete this step. The first responsibility of any new teacher must be to master the standard curriculum before determining how to modify it. At first, a teacher can complete the Unit Focus sheet at the completion of each unit. After a teacher feels at ease teaching the unit, these sheets can then be used to complete the Unit Curriculum Expansion sheet. Finally, the Yearly Project Sheet can be completed at the end of the school year in preparation for the following term.

Beginning slowly and adding new steps gradually helps teachers not to be overwhelmed by too many demands and too many new strategies. An easy method to utilize at the beginning of differentiated instruction is to start asking questions during class discussion using Bloom's Taxonomy. This leads naturally to more diversification of teaching and learning. As teachers become more confident in their abilities, they become more vested in the idea of differentiating instruction so that all students can benefit from the state standards of instruction and the traditional classroom curriculum in some form. Instead of "teaching towards the middle," teachers discover the joy of teaching to each child.

# 3

# STUDENTS WITH
# COGNITIVE IMPAIRMENTS

**D**ifferentiating instruction for students with Individual Educational Plans (IEPs) is actually easier than working with students with undiagnosed learning problems because the IEP determines the curriculum. The IEP serves as a road map to determine the educational goals for a student. The purpose of each lesson taught in the regular classroom is based on the child's IEP. The planning to determine this purpose should be a joint effort between the special educator and the classroom teacher. As discussed in rule #3, the regular educator is the expert in curriculum, and the special educator is the expert in special teaching methods. In order to determine the most important concepts for mastery of a unit, a teacher must be intimately involved with the curriculum. The classroom teacher, after at least one year of teaching, should be able to determine the most important aspects of the unit that should be included in instruction for the child with cognitive impairments. The special education teacher is best able to determine how to teach the child and whether this child is able to master these concepts. Collaboration between the regular educator and support staff, with role clarification, is necessary to develop a program jointly.

As an example of how a lesson can be modified to meet the needs of a child with moderate cognitive impairments, the seventh-grade science teacher and the special education teacher determined the following goals jointly. The rest of the class was required to do a five-page research paper as a culmination to the six-week "Environments" unit. The modified goals for the student with mild cognitive impairment included the student having an understanding of the following:

- Plants and animals live in the woods.
- Identification of two animals that live in the woods.
- Deserts are hot and dry.
- Identification of two animals that live in a desert.
- A pond is a small body of water.
- Identification of two animals that live in a pond.
- Oceans are large bodies of water.
- Identification of two animals that live in the ocean.

For assessment of this unit, the student was asked to identify pictures of woods, deserts, ponds, and oceans. In addition, this student was asked to make a book that matched animals to their correct environments. Thus, the student would master the essential concepts and could be included in class lectures and discussions. Although the goals for instruction and method of assessment are very different than for typical students in this class, the special learner is able to work side by side with a typical learner in a regular class.

The educational programs for students with more severe cognitive impairments should be based on the skills needed for independence at age twenty-one. These students should be taught to participate in common and regular daily routines. Their educational priorities are based on age-appropriate life skills. Instruction must include a functional curriculum—that is, a curriculum focusing on life skills. One of the functional curriculums often used is *The Syracuse Community-Referenced Curriculum Guide for Students with Moderate and Severe Disabilities* by Alison Ford, Roberta Schnorr, Luanna Meyer, Linda Davern, Jim Black, and Patrick Dempsey (Brooks Publishing). This curriculum includes scope and sequence instruction with specific tasks for children from three to twenty-one years of age. The content is divided into four curricular domains: self-management/home living, vocational, recreation/leisure, and general community functioning.

The self-management/home living domain includes domestic tasks such as eating, food preparation, grooming/dressing, hygiene/toileting, safety/health, caring for others, and budgeting/scheduling. Each of these goal areas is broken down into age-appropriate activities from pre-school through post–high school. Two types of skills are considered: those skills that are required or those that a student will be receiving (such as eating, toileting, and dressing) and those skills that are negotiable tasks (such as cooking, budgeting, and health). If a student has not mastered basic self-help skills before graduation, another person will forever be responsible for taking care of the student's basic needs. Certainly, skills in the first category must be a priority so that every student can be as independent as possible at age twenty-one. Negotiable skills in the second category are those skills that *someone* in a living arrangement must be able to do, but not essential for everyone to be able to do, such as money management, cooking, or laundry. Skill mastery in the first category enhances the quality of life for an individual, and therefore take precedence.

The purpose of teaching vocational skills at a young age and continuing instruction throughout a child's public education is to develop work attitudes and appropriate behaviors. A young child's vocational instruction includes a classroom or school job. A work ethic is taught whereby students learn that tasks must be completed in a timely and careful manner. Later, vocational instruction includes neighborhood or community jobs based on a student's interests and aptitudes. During the high school years, a student should experience a wide variety of jobs, such as housekeeping, laundry, lawn and garden, food service, clerical, industrial, and customer service. The goal is to help a student find a lifelong vocation by age twenty-one.

The recreation/leisure domain includes activities in which a student can engage either individually or with family or friends. Children with average cognitive abilities have many opportunities to decide what activities are relaxing for them. A child with a significant cognitive disability needs time within the school day to explore leisure options suited to the student's abilities. These activities begin with home leisure activities for young children and expand to community activities for older students. This is an important component of the educational plan for a student with cognitive impairments; therefore, it is appropriate to include instruction in recreational/leisure activities in the school setting. Typical children have many opportunities to determine preferences for recreational activities, whereas students with significant disabilities often are not exposed to a variety of leisure skills. Since at least one-third of a person's life is spent in activities other than working or sleeping, it is important that this domain be explored with each student.

The final domain of community instruction includes traveling, grocery shopping, general shopping, restaurant use, and community safety. Students with cognitive impairments learn best at the actual site where the skill normally occurs. Simulating a grocery store within a classroom does not transfer the student's skill to a real grocery store. The student must be taken into the community and experience the task of accessing services where they normally occur. A community bus shared between schools is an effective method of providing community instruction. A teacher aide or special education teacher can accompany the student to a fast-food restaurant or grocery store to teach the student how to order in a restaurant or fill a grocery list. A young child needs infrequent visits to the community, whereas a high school student needs frequent visits with increasing responsibilities while in the community.

Embedded within daily activities is instruction in social, communication, and motor areas. Students with cognitive impairments need direct instruction and practice in the area of social competence. They need to learn how to age-appropriately interact with peers. Depending on the significance of the cognitive impairment, adaptations may need to be made, such as physical adaptations for a student with cerebral palsy or an augmentative communication device for a student with severe speech impairment.

Motor instruction also occurs incidentally in functional contexts. Occupational therapy and physical therapy within the school setting are delivered through functional meaning, such as working on range of motion exercises during dressing activities or fine motor skills during eating tasks. The functional outcome of motor skills becomes the priority rather than a clinical model of isolated muscle tasks.

Communication skills are also taught throughout the functional curriculum. Staff members determine how a child with significant speech/language impairments can adapt to a situation by using augmentative communication systems such as object, photo, drawn picture symbols (picsyms), or written word communication. Gestures, vocalizations, facial expressions, body movement, blinking, or sign language are also viewed as possible forms of communication.

Finally, functional academics of time, money, reading, and writing instruction are also embedded in the functional curriculum. Students are taught the skills of telling time, making change, and functional reading and writing. These skills are taught as they relate to a student's ability to become as independent as possible. An academic reading vocabulary is not as meaningful or useful to a student with cognitive impairments as a reading program that stresses words seen in everyday living activities, such as brand names, emergency signage, and recipe ingredients. These functional academics are based on the student's current level of performance and cognitive ability.

Some community living activities may be included within the existing classroom curriculum. Food preparation can easily be integrated into a home economics class while personal hygiene can be included in the physical education portion of instruction. At other times, the individual goals of instruction for a student with special needs may be different from the goals for typical students in the classroom. For example, during a classroom discussion, the goals for other students may be to participate in interactive problem solving of an engaged learning activity (for example, How to best transport crops efficiently from southern states to northern states in a timely fashion). While the purpose of this lesson for other students is to compare the cost and efficiency of different transportation systems, the student with special needs may be learning how to appropriately participate in a group discussion, take turns, or work cooperatively. These skills cannot be taught to a student in isolation, but only by participating with his peer group.

At other times, instruction may need to take place outside of the regular classroom. Food preparation may need cooking facilities. Community instruction must take place within the community at restaurants, grocery stores, or recreational areas. By understanding that the IEP drives the student's curriculum, additional time may be spent during free periods to allow the special student to independently complete standard activities, such as gathering materials, changing clothes, toileting, etc. Such a student may need to enter the lunchroom earlier than other students so that she can prepare for lunch independently. It is important that teachers determine the most important educational needs and have those needs determine where, when, and what is taught.

Students with cognitive impairments need a balance between modified standard curriculum and specialized functional curriculum. Because their educational needs are so unique, their program must also be unique. Initially, students with significant cognitive needs can participate in most of the standard curriculum through differentiation. However, as the student gets older, the amount of modification required can often make the standard curriculum meaningless.

> Rule #6
> The older the child, the bigger the gap.

The standard kindergarten curriculum can meet the educational needs of most students. It is language rich and experiential. Much of instruction is dedicated to hands-on activities. But as the child ages, the curriculum becomes more abstract and requires higher levels of thinking to be meaningful. The gap between the learning needs of the typical child and the educational needs of a child with special needs widens. The child who was fully included in the kindergarten curriculum may need significant adaptations to be included in the fourth-grade curriculum. The older child's educational needs may not be adequately met through only an academic approach. It is important that parents know early that these changes in instruction will occur. By high school, students with significant cognitive impairments often need the majority of instruction spent on a functional curriculum. Standard algebra has little meaning and relevance, whereas instruction in money usage has a direct effect on the child's ability to be independent in the future.

> Rule #7
> Always begin with the end in mind.
> —Stephen Covey

As a child with cognitive impairments ages and the curriculum changes, teachers must determine what aspects are most valuable for the student to learn. Staff must continually ask the questions "How will this instruction positively affect the future for this student? Will this instruction help this student to function more independently as an adult?" The answers to these questions helps to determine instruction in both academic and functional areas. An individually designed program incorporating the best of the regular classroom instruction teamed with opportunities for functional curricular instruction will meet the unique educational needs of each student.

**4**

# CHILDREN WITH DIFFICULTIES
# ATTENDING TO TASK

There are very few teachers who would say that they have never worked with a child with attentional difficulties. Some students are medically diagnosed as having attention deficit disorder (ADD). Other children have been diagnosed with attention deficit with hyperactivity disorder (ADHD). And there are still even more children within a classroom who have difficulties staying on task but who have no medical or educational diagnosis. Attention deficit disorder and attention deficit with hyperactivity disorder are both neurological disorders clinically determined using neuropsychological testing, observation, teacher/parent questionnaires, and child interviews. Although clinical diagnosis is made through a member of the medical profession, many children demonstrate the characteristics of attentional difficulties and are never seen by a doctor. The most common characteristics of children with attentional challenges include inattention, impulsivity, and hyperactivity (Flick 1998).

Children with difficulty focusing attempt to attend to every stimulus around them. They have problems sifting through those stimuli that are important and those that can distract them from learning. These children can often attend to the correct material when they are in a one-to-one setting or in a room with few distractions.

Children with impulsivity concerns "act first, think later." They know the difference between right and wrong but make hasty decisions with respect to their own behavior, thus causing social problems. This impulsivity also affects their ability to learn because they may choose answers on a test without thinking carefully or they impatiently blurt out answers during classroom discussions.

Children with ADHD are easily recognized because their hyperactive behavior interferes with both their learning ability and social interactions. These children appear unable to sit quietly and attend to one topic for a developmentally appropriate length of time. They often jump from one activity to another, becoming bored easily. They seem to be in constant motion, either by gross motor activities of jumping, running, or skipping, or by more covert actions such as continually tapping their fingers or toes. This continued activity interferes with learning because these students have a difficult time remaining on task long enough to complete learning or assessment.

A typical lament from teachers is that these children "knew the information yesterday but aren't demonstrating that knowledge today." There are two main reasons why ADD children demonstrate this trait: either they haven't put the information into long-term memory initially or they can't find the information that has been placed in long-term memory. The brain of an ADD child can be compared to a Rolodex file. The information is "written" on a file card in memory, but those cards have not been alphabetized or sorted according to category. When asked to relay the information previously learned, the ADD child is unable to "stop the Rolodex file at the right card" to retrieve the information. The files keep spinning. This leads to disorganization in many areas of an ADD child's life. No systematic approach is used to organize materials, possessions, time or dates of appointments, or learned information.

How can a teacher help children with attentional concerns learn better? The first area of consideration must be the child's organizational ability.

---

Rule #8
The more disorganized the child is internally,
the more structured the learning
environment must be.

A teacher needs to develop a highly structured learning environment where a child knows what to expect in terms of time, learning expectations, and behavioral requirements. The teacher needs to help the child develop a routine that will compensate for the child's inability to organize himself. An arrival checklist placed next to a student's locker helps a child to organize the morning routine into manageable "chunks." Color-coding all materials needed for a specific class with the same color assists the child in being prepared. A child with organizational problems needs direct instruction on the use of an assignment notebook or day planner to include every assignment, appointment, event, or special dates.

---

Rule #9
Visual cues are easier to remove
than verbal cues.

---

A written arrival checklist is much more effective for learning than an adult verbally telling a child each day how to organize materials. For example, a mother of a young ADD child placed a morning checklist in the bathroom listing morning responsibilities such as brushing teeth, combing hair, washing face. Next to the back door was another list with afternoon responsibilities such as emptying backpack, placing notes on counter, and putting lunchbox in sink. It was the child's responsibility to check off tasks when completed. After a few months, the child removed the checklists because she had made them part of her daily routine. This same person is a now young adult and still relies on a day planner and sticky notes to keep on top of appointments and deadlines. With continued instruction in compensatory strategies, she was able to develop her own techniques as an adult.

Three reasons why children, especially those with ADD, do not hand in their homework include: they don't take home the materials; they do not do the homework; or they do not give the completed homework to the teacher. Unfortunately, teachers cannot control whether a child does or does not complete homework at home—but teachers can assist with the other two problems. A schoolwide system of student check-outs is one way to ensure that every child takes home the necessary materials for completing homework. Every staff member who is not a classroom teacher is assigned a classroom with which to work at the end of the school day. Throughout the day, teachers must write assignments on their boards. The support staff checks this board at the end of the day and asks all children on "check-outs" to come to the hallway with needed materials and backpack. The staff member then checks each child to make sure the assignment book is properly completed and that all necessary materials, including textbook, spiral notebook, worksheets, and so forth, are in the student's backpack. If the student has forgotten anything, she must return to the classroom, gather needed materials, and return to the end of the checkout line. In the morning, the teacher checks that homework is handed in. If parents are available and willing, it is of great benefit that they sign the assignment book as projects are completed and placed in the child's backpack. This procedure can be used with any child, regardless of learning abilities or disabilities. If the child is able to complete the sequence for two weeks with no reminders and hands in homework on time for two weeks with no reminders, the child is taken off check-outs. Many students actually request to be part of this checkout process because it makes them feel more secure and organized.

Junior high schools can benefit from a modified checkout program. Teachers end teaching two minutes before the end of each period. Students are asked to write the assignment for that subject in their assignment books. The teacher quickly circulates the room, stamping his initials on the correct assignment. Students with significant organizational problems are assigned a staff member to check them out at the end of the day to ensure that they have each assignment stamped by the teacher as well as the correct materials to complete each assignment. Many high schools have used this system in the beginning of high school to help students become organized. As the school year continues, only those students with significant concerns continue to have their assignment books checked by each teacher.

Classroom teachers must also realize that children with ADD or ADHD do not choose to be hyperactive or not pay attention. Therefore, teachers must "pick their battles" carefully. If it is important that the child concentrate on instruction, then it probably will not affect learning if the child jiggles a foot or stands during instruction. The child may be able to pay attention for short periods of time but require frequent breaks. These breaks can be as short as the time needed to sharpen a pencil or have a drink of water. Many teachers have found that allowing a child a predetermined number of breaks within a specified period of time allows the child flexibility as well as ensuring adequate learning time. The child may be given three breaks consisting of thirty seconds each within a forty-five-minute period. When those three breaks have occurred, the child must remain seated. It is the child's responsibility to use the breaks when really needed. The number of breaks can be gradually reduced as the child matures. How the breaks are used can be jointly decided between the student and teacher.

To help keep a child focused requires many different techniques. The student may need to change tasks frequently. This can be done by giving the student all the assignments for a morning and allowing the student to change between assignments throughout the morning. Although the eventual goal would be to have the child complete one task at a time, the initial variety may keep attention focused longer. Permitting postural variety can also assist in focusing. Allowing the child to stand at her desk while completing seatwork or sit creatively (kneeling, cross-legged on chair) may alleviate the discomfort of remaining still. The teacher must decide priorities for students with attentional concerns. If completing work and mastering the curriculum are the priorities for the student, then how the student stands or the number of necessary breaks are insignificant. Modifications may be necessary, but the top concern is the child's ability to meet full potential.

Although children with ADHD are often easy to identify due to their constant motion, the child with ADD can often be overlooked. These children can appear sluggish, disorganized, and inconsistent. They often have little awareness of time. They are mistakenly called daydreamers. It appears that they are choosing to think about activities other than the task at hand. It is important to remember that ADD is a neurological impairment just as ADHD is neurologically based. These children are not choosing to be distracted. Their impulses are stronger than their ability to maintain focus. One method of initial identification of students with ADD is the slow response time. Going back to the "Rolodex theory," a child with ADD has previously learned information but is unable to stop the Rolodex quickly. Given additional response time, the child with ADD will generally have the correct response. The child needs uninterrupted extended time (possibly twenty seconds) to sort the information and complete the answer. A child with a slower response time who generally discovers the correct answer may have attentional deficit concerns.

One of the most important general teaching techniques for successfully working with students with attentional difficulties is to establish a clear routine along with clearly defined rules, expectations, and consequences, in a classroom with few distractions. These students need to know exactly what is expected of them and what is needed to be successful. When directions are given, it is often helpful to have the student repeat the directions back to the teacher to ensure proper understanding. Smooth transitions teamed with cues of changing activities can ease disruption. Private signals between the teacher and student that help remind the student of appropriate behavior can be effective as can proximity control and preferential seating. A nonverbal touch on the shoulder or pointing to the proper stimuli can help the student remain focused. One teacher used a neon-colored paper plate that she directed to her face to help an ADD student focus on her verbal instructions. Although the other students understood the reason behind the paper plate, the teacher could continue instruction without verbal interruption.

When it is believed that the child is capable of remaining on task better than he is demonstrating, a response cost system may be necessary. Natural consequences for not completing work on an agreed schedule are effective. This may include loss of privileges or additional work to be completed for homework. Reprimands need to be brief and given in a calm, firm voice. It is important to constantly reevaluate the child's ability to complete tasks to make sure expectations are realistic. The use of behavioral charts and contracts are visual reminders of progress and often reinforcers themselves. In table 4.1, the similarities and differences between students with attentional deficit disorder and students with attention deficit disorder with hyperactivity are compared. In most ways, these students are very similar and educational strategies are very comparable.

**Table 4.1.    Differences and Similarities of ADD and ADHD**

|  | ADD | ADHD |
|---|:---:|:---:|
| Attend to every stimulus, meaningful and nonmeaningful | X | X |
| Impulsive | X | X |
| Uneven learning patterns: learn a concept one day and forget it the next day | X | X |
| Disorganization | X | X |
| Inability to maintain attention | X | X |
| Memory problems | X | X |
| Appears to be daydreaming | X |  |
| Hyperactive |  | X |
| Learns best with visual cues to help remember daily routine | X | X |
| Benefits from clear routine | X | X |
| Needs clear directions and expectations | X | X |

Students with attentional deficits can be challenging. It is the teacher's responsibility to make the classroom welcoming and accommodating for all students. The use of humor and genuine concern can help alleviate tension and build the student's self-confidence. Regardless of conflicts during the previous day, the student must know that each day begins with a fresh slate. Each day is a new opportunity for success.

**5**

# STUDENTS WITH LEARNING DISABILITIES AND STUDENTS IDENTIFIED AS SLOW LEARNERS

**W**hy would students with learning disabilities be grouped in this book with students identified as slow learners? Unfortunately, many teachers believe that these two categories are interchangeable. They are not. Although both groups of students need special methodology for learning and some of those methods overlap, it is imperative that teachers understand how different the educational needs are for each. In this chapter, the learning needs of children with learning disabilities are discussed, followed by educational strategies for slow learners, and a comparison of methods and strategies for both groups of students.

## STUDENTS WITH LEARNING DISABILITIES

A learning disability affects a person's ability to either interpret what he sees and hears, or to link information from different parts of the brain (National Institutes of Health 1993). Manifestations may include difficulties with spoken and written language, coordination, attention, memory, or visual or auditory perceptual difficulties. By definition, these students have at least average intelligence and have no emotional, physical, visual acuity, hearing acuity, or environmental/cultural problems primarily responsible for learning difficulties. A severe discrepancy exists between the student's intellectual ability and the student's academic achievement. The student may be showing difficulties in written language, reading, or math although having average or above-average intelligence.

How can a child have normal visual acuity and have visual perceptual difficulties? Visual acuity pertains to the shape of the eyeball and, therefore, a person's ability to see objects clearly. Visual perception refers to a person's ability to understand or interpret what is seen. The visual information goes through the eye properly, but a breakdown occurs in the brain's ability to process what the eye sees. This often takes the form of letter reversals or visual disorganization—the inability to sort and use what is seen. This may manifest in a figure-ground disorder, which is difficulty focusing on the significant feature rather than the background distractions. Children with visual-memory problems have difficulties remembering information that is presented visually.

These same problems can occur in the auditory processing ability. A child's hearing is normal, but how the brain processes what is heard is impaired. The student may be unable to discriminate sounds or have difficulties blocking out irrelevant sounds from important messages. Other students demonstrate learning concerns when they are required to process auditory information quickly. Their "processing speed" may be deficient. And, as with the visual area, auditory memory difficulties can make remembering information presented verbally difficult.

Other symptoms that can be present with a learning disability include tactile defensiveness (highly sensitive to tactile stimulation), visual-motor integration (both visual and motor systems work well independently, but not together), sequencing (reproducing in order), memory (both long term and short term), and difficulties with learning abstract information.

The "at least average intelligence" component of learning disabilities is where the breakdown in communication often occurs. Teachers often think that a child with a learning disability is "mildly cognitively impaired." Teachers may believe that the child with a learning disability is unable to learn. These misperceptions can negatively affect how a child with a learning disability is educated. Children with learning disabilities have the ability to learn the standard curriculum, but they must be taught using special methodologies in order to circumvent their specific learning challenge. Their average or above-average intelligence means that they must be challenged to use higher-level thinking skills while given opportunities to demonstrate their knowledge in unconventional means.

Education for learning-disabled students was the responsibility of the LD resource teacher when learning disabilities originally became a recognized category of special education. Students were pulled out of their regular classes to receive special assistance in another room. There was often little connection between what was taught in the LD room and what was taught in the classroom. Today, differentiated instruction has made it possible for students with learning disabilities to be educated within the classroom with support services "pushed in" by the resource teacher. A new role having three primary responsibilities has been established for the resource teacher: to tutor the student in the standard curriculum, to remediate deficient skill areas, and to teach study/metacognition skills.

As a tutor, the resource teacher assists the student with completing assignment, studying for tests, and understanding the content areas. Students with learning disabilities often need extended time or a quiet place for working or testing. The resource teacher can provide this area while also reinforcing the concepts taught in class. When the learning disability is severe, the resource teacher must work collaboratively with the classroom teacher to determine the core concepts that must be taught to the student and which concepts are not essential to learning.

Another role for the LD teacher is to help remediate the skill weaknesses of the child. Instruction in phonics, comprehension, math facts, or writing syntax is a necessary component of a specialized program. Because the basic skill levels for students with learning disabilities often lag behind their peers, these students need to continue instruction in the content areas while receiving specialized instruction in basic skills. This instruction must be individualized to meet the specific needs of each student. If a student did not learn how to read properly using a standard basal series in the first place, continued use of standard strategies is not effective. These students need a multisensory approach to learning basic skills, teamed with a highly structured method called *direct instruction*.

Direct instruction requires the teacher to break down large learning tasks into small sequential steps. Each of these steps must be taught as concretely as possible in a highly organized manner that the student can reproduce on her own. Direct instruction leaves nothing to chance. Each part of a skill is specifically taught until the student demonstrates mastery. For example, phonics instruction is broken into very tiny components such as "long 'e' words." Through a series of specific tasks, opportunities for practice, and assessment, the child is taught this microcomponent of the task of reading. Plenty of practice and scheduled review is offered. Students may be taught some skills in isolation but then must be always taught how to integrate these small tasks into the larger picture. Table 5.1 shows the major components of direct instruction.

When a teacher is utilizing direct instruction to teach a task, the teacher begins instruction by modeling how to complete the task. Because teacher directions are minimized, the student is prompted to complete the task more independently until all teacher assistance is eliminated. Students with learning challenges need frequent guided practice to keep the skill fresh and to aid in transferring the skill into long-term memory. This prescribed routine in learning helps the student in a highly structured setting to learn how to use the "rules" of learning. The goal is to begin with guaranteed success, having the teacher model and prompt, and gradually decrease assistance as the student becomes more confident in task completion.

The third role of the resource teacher is to use direct instruction to teach the skills of metacognition and learning strategies. Metacognition is developing an understanding of how one learns. A person without learning challenges develops a personal learning style that is effective for that person. A child with a learning disability must be taught the spe-

**Table 5.1.  Direct Instruction**

Never leave anything to chance.
Use a systematic "recipe" method for learning.
Teach strategies and provide generalization.

- Modeling
- Prompting
- Frequent Guided Practice
- Frequent Positive Feedback
- Prescribed Routine in Learning
- Instruction in How to Use the Rules
- Gradual Fading of Assistance

cific skills necessary to make that child an effective learner. Some skills included in metacognition include (Deshler, Ellis, and Lenz 1996):

- Activating background knowledge
- Predicting
- Self-questioning
- Visualizing
- Summarizing
- Monitoring comprehension
- Prioritizing
- Comparing current learning to previous knowledge
- Looking for patterns of information
- Organizing learned material

Students need to know how to reflect upon and evaluate incoming information. They need to understand how to approach a problem-solving activity and how to monitor their own progress during this activity. Teachers, both classroom and resource, must equip these children with a repertoire of learning strategies and systematic steps to follow when working through a learning task. The ultimate goal of metacognitive instruction is self-regulation, such as goal setting, self-instruction, self-monitoring, and self-reinforcement (Graham, Harris, and Reid 1992). Students who are able to determine how to learn and then evaluate the effectiveness of their chosen strategy are successful in new learning situations.

Learning strategies are the tools and techniques a learner uses to understand and learn new material (Alley and Deshler 1979; Lenz, Ellis, and Scanlon 1996; Deshler and Shumaker 1986). Learning strategies can include taking notes, asking questions, studying for a test, making an outline, or organizing materials. The classroom teacher can provide naturally occurring opportunities to utilize learning strategies. The teacher can first teach the strategy using direct instruction, demonstrate its usefulness, model using this strategy, allow time for practicing a specific strategy, and finally include periodic reinforcement and review of learned strategies. Feedback to the students regarding the effectiveness of their use of the strategy is important. The essence of Deshler and Shumaker's learning strategies is summarized in tables 5.2 and 5.3.

Strategies utilizing metacognition are more executory in nature, requiring higher levels of thinking. These strategies include planning,

**Table 5.2.   Principles of Learning Strategies
(Deshler and Shumaker 1986)**

- Demand students' involvement
- Identify and teach prerequisite skills
- Learn the strategy
- Recognize and reward student effort
- Require mastery
- Integrate instruction
- Provide direct explanation
- Promote generalization

monitoring, and evaluating one's own learning. Children with learning disabilities need direct instruction on how to go about the task of learning. Each person has a personal repertoire of skills that enables him to learn effectively. Each person has learning weaknesses that make learning in a specific manner more challenging. A person with well-developed skills of metacognition is able to focus on learning strengths and compensate for learning weaknesses. Students who have mastered the strategies of predicting, planning, checking, and monitoring are active learners who take responsibility for their academic growth. Teachers can use table 5.4 as a quick reminder of the components of metacognition instruction.

Meichenbaum (1975) used the idea of direct instruction to train students in the principles of metacognition. First, teachers must model the components of metacognition, talking out loud as they perform the strategies. Next, the teacher performs the same task while modeling the behavior and prompting the student. The third step involves having the student whisper the directions to herself while completing the task independently. Finally, the student is able to perform the task while internalizing the directions. Again, frequent guided practice is necessary. Table 5.5 can be

**Table 5.3.   Types of Learning Strategies
(Deshler and Shumaker 1986)**

- Organizational strategies: logs, charts, color-coding, sticky notes
- Time management strategies: planners, timers, calendars, alarm watches
- Memory strategies: mnemonics, categorizing, chunking
- Test-taking strategies: directions, checking, skimming
- Social skill strategies: conversation, cooperation, listening
- Speech strategies: formal presentations
- Handwriting strategies: posture, grip, position, stroke
- Homework strategies: planning, follow-through, organization

**Table 5.4.  Metacognition: Knowing How to Go about the Task of Learning**

- Awareness of one's own systematic thinking about learning
- Helping oneself learn and remember
- Understanding and using the principles of effective studying
- Understanding one's own limitations and how to compensate for these limitations
- Self-monitoring and making adjustments as needed.
- Strategies
  - predicting
  - planning
  - checking
  - monitoring
- Defies passive learning

posted in the classroom to help the teacher and the students remember the steps for metacognition.

How can a classroom teacher best work with a child with a learning disability? Collaboration and shared responsibility between the classroom teacher and the LD teacher are essential. As previously stated, the classroom teacher is the expert in curriculum and therefore must determine the essential skills for each unit of study. Depending on the severity of the learning disability, some students will only master the essential skills while other students with learning disabilities will go far beyond the standard curriculum in both depth and breadth. Either way, the classroom teacher must plan for, teach, and assess the student with a learning disability cooperatively with the resource teacher, who is the expert in special methods for teaching these students.

Classroom teachers can help students become more effective learners by helping them become organized, by modeling learning strategies while teaching, and by working through systematic steps to follow when completing a learning task. As specific learning strategies are taught through direct instruction, frequent opportunities to practice and use these strategies are essential. Providing activities that allow students to practice and discuss strategies with peers is helpful.

**Table 5.5.  Training Steps for Metacognition**

- Adult models while talking out loud.
- Student does same task while teacher models behavior and speaks directions.
- Student whispers direction while completing the task.
- Student performs the task while internalizing directions.

—Meichenbaum 1975

Kameenui and Simmons (1999) summarized six principles of effective curriculum design: concentration on "big idea," conspicuous strategy instruction, mediated scaffolding, guided practice, linkage of concepts, and judicious review. These principles benefit instruction to all students but are particularly useful for classrooms that include students with learning disabilities. The first principle states that teachers need to concentrate on the "big ideas" by determining the essential concepts (based on state standards), initially focusing on those concepts, and gradually proceeding with more complex ideas as the student become more proficient.

Students benefit when the teacher models conspicuous strategies. Similar to direct instruction, conspicuous strategy instruction communicates explicitly the steps a learner must complete to accomplish a task. Students are taught a "set of rules" to follow in order to achieve an academic goal, such as steps to be taken when a word is unfamiliar in a passage.

A third principle of effective curriculum design is mediated scaffolding. When a concept is first introduced, unnecessary verbiage or extraneous information is eliminated in order to assist student learning. Initially, instruction is teacher-directed in a systematic fashion. Tasks are sequenced to progress from simple to complex as student understanding increases. As students master the basic concepts, higher-level concepts are then introduced, linking the major ideas within the curriculum. Guided practice is offered to allow the student to slowly absorb more complexities of the task. The goal is to eliminate teacher-guided class work and lead to student-directed activity completion.

It is imperative that students with learning disabilities have plenty of opportunity for what Kameenui calls judicious review. As new concepts are introduced, students need planned activities to reinforce previous learning and assist with recall. These reviews must be structured and offered at regular intervals.

Children with learning disabilities often appear to be "underachievers," which means that they are not performing to their intellectual capabilities. Teachers must realize that these students have at least average intelligence and the ability to utilize higher levels of thinking. At the same time, teachers must also realize that learning is difficult for these students due to their processing deficits. Differentiation of instruction and working through the student's learning strengths while remaining cognizant of the student's learning deficits allows the student with a learning disability to reach his full potential. This task requires flexibility and creativity on the part of the teacher. Lessons must be fast moving, multisensory, and stimulating.

In summary, students with learning disabilities have the cognitive ability to learn and remember the standard curriculum. However, this cognitive ability is negatively affected by the student's learning difficulties in the areas of language, perception, attention, memory, or coordination. Students with learning disabilities need to be taught methodically while being challenged to meet full potential.

## STUDENTS IDENTIFIED AS SLOW LEARNERS

In comparison, students who have been diagnosed as slow learners have less-than-average intellectual ability, with IQs generally between seventy and eighty-five. These students learn approximately 85 percent slower than their peers, with their achievement commensurate with their ability. Children with lower IQs learn at a steady rate of progress, especially rote facts, but demonstrate great difficulties with abstract concepts. These students also have problems transferring learning. They may utilize skills aptly in the classroom but be unable to replicate the skills outside of the classroom. Unfortunately, these students do not qualify for special education services, but they struggle to cope with the academic demands of the regular classroom (Carroll 1998). Slow learners can be misidentified as lazy, unmotivated, or stubborn. In order to adequately design an educational program to specifically meet their needs, a teacher should refer a student for a full psychological exam and case study, to ensure that another learning problem is not causing the learning difficulties.

The three major components of teaching slow learners include making the abstract concrete, assisting with generalization difficulties, and working toward automaticity of basic concepts (Shaw 1999). These students work best using concrete, hands-on manipulation of objects. Paper-and-pencil activities are abstract and difficult to grasp. Giving visual cues and manipulatives during paper-and-pencil activities can help abstract concepts become more concrete. Generalization only occurs when a skill has been practiced and reinforced so many times that it has become internalized for the learner. Once internalized, timed practice helps to automate these skills. By encouraging speed of response, skills become automated.

While students with learning disabilities need challenging, fast-paced, multisensory instruction, students who are slow learners need repetition in a highly structured learning environment. These students need three to five times as much repetition as a typical learner does in order for a learned task to become automatic. They need opportunities to practice skills and specific instruction on how to generalize those skills to other learning arenas. Because abstract learning is so difficult for these students, concrete instruction using manipulatives and concrete examples is essential. This instruction will require follow-up review and time for practice. A general rule of thumb when working with students who are slow learners is to slow the pace of instruction, vary instruction as little as possible on a single task, and provide plenty of practice. Initially, the practice should take place in the same setting, in as structured an environment as possible. In order to assist with generalization difficulties, practice eventually will need to be modified to help the child use the skill in a variety of settings.

In addition, students identified as slow learners need shorter assignments in order to guarantee success. Students who are slow learners work at a slower rate and therefore take longer to complete assignments. Insisting that these students complete the same number of math problems or homework assignments as other nonchallenged students frustrates the child and does not help her to develop positive self-esteem as a learner. Breaking up large assignments into small portions allows the student to feel successful as each component is completed.

Again, the classroom teacher must determine the essential concepts of each unit of instruction. Students who are slow learners need to develop a basic understanding of new concepts that will be relevant to future learning. Just as a computer disk has only so much storage space, the student who is a slow learner has limited learning ability. Teachers must ensure that key concepts and core curriculum are mastered.

## TEACHING STRATEGIES

For both students with learning disabilities and students identified as slow learners, many teaching strategies apply. Utilizing visual and auditory cues simultaneously during instruction allows a child to pick his best learning style. At the same time, teachers must be careful to eliminate as many distracters as possible. It is especially important that the teacher not distract from the learning activity by using too much verbalization. Teachers need to present directions and instruction succinctly and then allow for extended processing time with no interruptions. Because teachers want so desperately to teach, they often use too much verbalization, afraid that "dead air time" is detrimental to students. Just the opposite is true. All students, particularly students with learning disabilities and students who are slow learners, appreciate a few quiet moments to reflect upon current learning. This quiet time allows newly learned information to be stored properly in long-term memory.

Table 5.6 shows the similarities and differences between students with learning disabilities and students who are diagnosed as slow learners. Table 5.7 demonstrates how instruction can be effectively differentiated for each type of learner. The most important difference is that students with learning disabilities have average or above-average intelligence and need to be intellectually challenged while allowing for processing deficits. Slow learners have below-average intelligence and will

**Table 5.6. Differences/Similarities of Slow Learners and Learning Disabilities**

|  | Slow Learner | LD |
|---|:---:|:---:|
| Below-average IQ | X |  |
| Average or above-average IQ |  | X |
| Achievement commensurate with ability | X |  |
| Achievement behind ability |  | X |
| Will always lag behind peers academically | X |  |
| Has cognitive ability to be at grade level academically |  | X |
| Uneven learning patterns; learns a concept one day and forgets it the next day |  | X |
| Disorganization | X | X |
| Inability to maintain attention |  | X |
| Memory problems |  | X |
| Learns best with repetition | X |  |
| Needs variety in presentation format: visual, kinesthetic, auditory, tactile |  | X |
| Benefits from clear routine | X | X |
| Needs clear directions and expectations | X | X |
| Learns best with visual cues to help remember daily routine | X | X |
| Benefit from instruction in metacognition and learning strategies | X | X |

Table 5.7.    Methods of Instruction (LD and Slow Learner)

|  | LD | Slow Learner | Both |
|---|---|---|---|
| CONTENT | Can learn entire curriculum in incremental steps; Needs challenging higher-level thinking tasks | Begin instruction at current level core concepts; Below grade level; Academic gap widens with age | Determine essential concepts |
| PROCESS | Direct instruction Systematic review Multimodality instruction; Needs variety of instruction | Instruction at literal or comprehension level; Repetition; Review; Keep instruction consistent | Systematic instruction; Integrate technology Specific instructions Guided practice Keep self-confidence as a learner high; Reduce distractions; Teach and practice learning strategies Use visuals and manipulatives; Needs meaningful, concrete activities; Simplify directions and check for understanding; Begin with previously learned knowledge |
| PRODUCT | Adaptations needed for deficit areas, such as writing, reading, | Based on core concepts to be mastered; Simplify or shorten | Based on purpose of instruction; Alternative assessment; Shorter tasks; Extended time; Quiet place; Individual contracts |

never master all concepts at their designated grade level. Core concepts must be determined to ensure that the slow learners have mastered the most important part of the curriculum.

A highly structured classroom environment, where students know what is expected of them, where a predictable schedule is generally followed, where directions and assignments are clearly stated, and where instruction is differentiated to meet the individual needs of students ensures that students with learning disabilities and students who are slow learners meet their fullest potential.

# 6

# CHILDREN WHOSE NATIVE LANGUAGE IS NOT ENGLISH

Children from families whose primary language is not English represent an increasing percentage of students enrolled in schools. The effectiveness of different programs to educate these students has been debated. Many educators feel that students learning English as a second language (ESL) should be pulled out of the classrooms and taught English through specific methodologies. Other experts believe that students learn best when educated alongside their English-speaking peers, using the standard curriculum as a basis for instruction. In either case, classroom teachers must plan to differentiate instruction for ESL students. The amount and depth of the modifications will be based on the student's level of understanding or usage of English, previous learning, and cognitive ability.

A second language is acquired in much the same way that the first language is acquired: through meaningful interactions with others. The ESL student has a broad base of experiences and vocabulary on which to build, although in another language. This base is an established system of language, with grammar, vocabulary, and sounds. Therefore, an ESL student learns English differently than does an infant learning English for the first time.

Krashen and Terrell (1983) describe how second language acquisition takes place. In the beginning of learning another language, students begin to understand messages in their new language. Bits and pieces of target vocabulary are comprehensible to them. As more vocabulary is understood, the child begins to focus on what is being said rather than how it is being said. Because so much effort is being expended on understanding each word, little attention can be given to the meaning behind the message. Therefore, students are unable to pick up on subtle forms of body language, intonation, or humor. Students are acting on a strictly literal level of comprehension. The next step of language acquisition enables the student to begin having meaningful communication in a second language. The second language can now be used for communicating ideas rather than individual words. Krashen calls the final level of acquisition "low affective filter," in which the learner has some degree of self-confidence in understanding and using the new language. Learners are now comfortable using the second language.

According to Krashen and Terrell (1983), four levels of English acquisition are generally acknowledged in school systems. A student with level 1 skills is at the preproduction stage and is developing survival vocabulary. This child is beginning to understand patterns, sounds, and the rhythm of English. Most student responses at this level are nonverbal and include pointing, gesturing, nodding, or drawing. When teaching a child at this level, a teacher should provide opportunities for active listening, use of visuals, and use of real objects for learning and expressing. Any new concept that can be demonstrated visually will be easier for the child to master. Students at this level should be encouraged to speak in English, yet not forced prematurely. Classroom instruction needs to be highly modified at this level.

At level 2, or the early speech production stage, students are beginning to develop reading and writing skills. They are able to use routine expressions and small phrases independently. They are able to listen with greater understanding and demonstrate an increased confidence in learning. At this stage, students are able to recognize the written version of their oral vocabulary. Teachers must continue to provide opportunity for listening comprehension with visual support. Teachers can begin to ask literal levels of questions, particularly "yes/no" and "who/what/where when/why" questions. This is the time to have students label pictures and objects to expand their vocabulary. The student's primary language is still the language of choice for content learning.

By level 3, the speech emergence stage, students are developing an academic vocabulary and speaking in longer phrases, although grammatically incorrect. They begin to participate more in class discussions and use writing in English to communicate. Reading ability increases although oral fluency is difficult. Teachers should continue to focus on communication, yet be careful not to correct or intimidate improper use of English grammar. Open-ended questions at higher levels of Bloom's Taxonomy can be used at this level. Reading and writing can be evaluated in a more grade-level appropriate manner, stressing student strengths and progress. Reading materials that require higher-level thinking skills should be offered to continue to enhance English development.

By level 4, the student is able to use extensive vocabulary, demonstrating a high level of accuracy and higher order thinking. Teachers need to provide opportunities for the student to use these newly acquired verbal and written skills. It is very important to note that it can take five to seven years for a child learning English to reach level 4. Many factors influence this timeline, such as parents' level of education, previous learning, and parents' use of English at home. Although students at lower levels of English acquisition appear to be able to use English in academic contexts, it is not until level 4 that a student is able to "think" in English and not translate questions and responses back and forth between English and her native language. Students at level 4 are now considered fluent in English.

Some general teaching strategies apply to all levels of language acquisition. When students first enter the U.S. educational system, they are generally fearful and hesitant. The most important task for the teacher is to make the child feel comfortable and welcome. This can be done through the use of a class buddy and daily one-to-one interaction with the teacher. It is imperative that the teacher and classmates pronounce the child's name correctly and learn something about the child's culture. The new student should be included in all activities with adjusted expectations. Initially, the student will experience a silent period that should be respected. At this time, the child should be given alternative activities or methods for communicating.

The teacher must help the student to master the subject matter while acquiring English proficiency. Abstract concepts need to be taught through concrete examples, with opportunities for students to hear and use meaningful language in real contexts. If possible, lessons should be previewed in the student's first language to facilitate the understanding of the concepts.

For all levels of second language acquisition, a teacher can help by speaking clearly and at a reasonable rate using simple consistent vocabulary (table 6.1). The teacher should stress the message and not the form in student responses, accepting grammatically incorrect responses and modeling the correct form. Individual clarification of assignments and directions will usually be necessary, especially during beginning acquisition.

If a bilingual or ESL teacher is available, the classroom teacher should share curriculum and classroom activities with this support staff member. This provides consistency of concepts and vocabulary and provides an opportunity for preteaching vocabulary and concepts. The bilingual or ESL teacher can often provide the student with the necessary background knowledge to make current learning meaningful.

**Table 6.1.   Second Language Acquisition and Content Instruction**

| Level | Characteristics | Strategies |
|---|---|---|
| **ONE–Preproduction State** | Does not speak or understand English<br>Has few phrases<br>Survival vocabulary<br>Silent period<br>Work highly modified | Nonverbal demonstrations needed<br>Abstract concepts made concrete<br>Build vocabulary |
| **TWO–Early Production** | Understands simple oral phrases<br>Speaks with hesitancy<br>Begins conversational speech<br>Work highly modified | Continue to build vocabulary<br>Listing/sorting/categorizing helpful<br>Nonverbal assessment of core concepts<br>Yes/no assessment |
| **THREE–Speech Emergence** | Understands parts of lessons<br>Reads and writes in second language at lower grade level<br>Work less modified | Activities to promote higher levels of language use<br>Stress emerging literacy<br>Continue to expand vocabulary<br>Begin extended assessment in English |
| **FOUR–Fluency** | Understands majority of instruction<br>May still be below grade level in reading and writing<br>Speaks and understands without difficulty | Focus of instruction is content areas<br>Reading and writing incorporated into instruction<br>Limited modifications needed |

When determining methods of assessment for classroom activities, the purpose is to allow students to show what they know. Standardized tests are a very poor measure of an ESL student's knowledge of the subject matter. Standardized tests are very language intensive, requiring a discriminating reader. Time limitations teamed with language nuances often confuse and frustrate ESL students, causing them to give up and mark random answers. Assessment alternatives could include teacher observation, portfolio assessment, and anecdotal records. The use of graphics and illustrations to clarify answers allows the student to concentrate on the subject matter. Tests translated into the native language allow the child to concentrate on the subject matter rather than language acquisition. Providing a pass/fail option at beginning stages of language acquisition allows the student to concentrate on the core concepts of instruction. Extended time for both tests and homework is often necessary. Table 6.2 summarizes alternative methods of assessment for students who are learning a second language.

Within the American system of teaching English as a second language, some educators believe that students learn English best if they are taught through the use of discrete, segregated skills. In the segregated skills model, the mastery of specific skills such as reading and speaking is separated from content learning (Mohan 1986). These skills are taught in isolation of other skills. Learning strategies for language acquisition can include cognitive and metacognitive training as well as grammar and vocabulary instruction.

In the segregated skills model, students are often taught learning strategies to help improve their progress in comprehending, internalizing, and using English (Oxford 1990). One strategy is metacognition, or understanding how one goes about the task of learning. Students who have well-developed metacognition skills are able to be cognizant of their thinking and reflective processes. Anderson (1999) believes the primary components of learning strategy instruction include preparing and planning for learning, selecting and using learning strategies, monitoring strategy use, orchestrating various strategies, and evaluating strategy use and learning.

Students who learn effectively are able to prepare and plan their methods for learning. This helps them determine what they need to know and how to go about accomplishing this goal. After preparing

**Table 6.2.    Alternative Assessment for ESL Students**

| Method | Description |
|---|---|
| Teacher Observation | • Teacher observes student and keeps anecdotal records on learning.<br>• Focuses on subject rather than English proficiency.<br>• Is both process and product oriented.<br>• Monitors progress without formal testing. |
| Student Portfolios | • Allows multi-modality demonstration on knowledge.<br>• Less threatening.<br>• Can be done in both native language and English.<br>• Focuses on content mastery. |
| Verbal Tests | • Verbal acquisition precedes written acquisition.<br>• No reading required.<br>• Less threatening.<br>• Allows teacher subjective evaluation. |
| Assessment in Native Language | • Allows total concentration on subject matter.<br>• Good for students at levels one and two.<br>• Must have staff member who speaks native language. |
| Pass/Fail Grading | • Allows teacher to concentrate on student's learning of core concepts.<br>• Good for students at levels one and two. |
| Extended Time | • Essential for beginning language acquisition.<br>• Minimizes anxiety.<br>• Truer example of student's best work. |
| Close Procedure | • Student fills in missing vocabulary word in a sentence.<br>• Good method to concentrate on subject matter vocabulary.<br>• Good for levels one and two. |
| Mapping | • Student is given a concept to map.<br>• Good assessment for beginning writing.<br>• Useful for core content assessment.<br>• Focuses on subject matter vocabulary. |

to learn, the student must select and use an appropriate learning strategy. This may include such ideas as specific reading strategies, strategies to overcome an unknown concept, effective writing strategies, or memorization techniques. Throughout learning, the student must then monitor the strategy to determine its effectiveness. No single strategy is effective in every learning situation, so students must understand how to orchestrate various strategies. They must be able to coordinate, organize, and make associations among different strategies. Students must possess the ability to switch from one strategy to another as necessary.

In comparison, the integrated-skill model utilizes content-based language instruction. Students practice all language skills in an integrated setting while learning content such as social studies, science, or math (Scarcella and Oxford 1992). This method emphasizes learning content through language. Students participate in structured learning experiences based on the content areas, with teachers and students modeling language use and providing opportunities for oral and written English practice.

There is a strong research base that supports the theory that the appropriate use of the native language is a powerful and effective tool for teaching (Lucas 1992). When students first enter the U.S. educational system, their own language is their only effective means for learning the classroom curriculum. By utilizing previous learning in the native language and combining these experiences with current instruction, the child is able to form relationships and understanding.

Fred Genesee (1995), with the National Center for Research on Cultural Diversity and Second Language Learning, stresses the importance of basic tenets in any ESL instruction. Genesee states that language instruction must be integrated with content instruction. Language learning results from using language to perform authentic communications. Language taught in meaningful and social contexts has more relevance and thus is a more effective learning context. Learning language during daily activities also ensures that second language usage will be generalized. As students are learning English, they should be encouraged to use their native language to aid in learning. If possible, children with similar language backgrounds should be placed in the same classroom to assist in learning. Parents and volunteers can be utilized to help use the native language when learning content areas.

The second tenet of effective instruction is the creation of a classroom environment that is rich in conversational opportunities. Students must have opportunities to practice and use the language they have learned with their peers and other people. This allows students to choose situations in which to use their newly acquired skills. Cooperative learning can facilitate this tenet. By grouping students for cooperative learning activities, the stress level is lowered, and students are able to become an active and integral part of the learning activity. ESL students are able to develop language and self-confidence.

Finally, effective second-language instruction includes language instruction systematically planned to correlate with content instruction. Time is allotted for presentation, practice, and application of specific language skills. Teachers need to model more complex language and stress higher-level thinking skills in English as a student progresses in English competency (Swain 1988). Salomone (1992) stresses the importance of using the second language while incorporating, planning, and teaching grammar and vocabulary.

As children learn English, a classroom teacher can assist in many ways. Teaching English through the content areas using activity-based learning while including instruction in new vocabulary is a tall order for any teacher. This task can be accomplished using methods readily available to the classroom teacher. The use of simple, consistent vocabulary helps the student to develop a better understanding of English. The use of visuals and manipulatives is of great importance. Posters, charts, pictures, and objects help bridge a language gap. Story mapping, word and picture cards, and graphics can be helpful when learning new concepts. Labeling and posting vocabulary throughout the school can help with learning the written word. When students are reading, the ESL child should have the same book as the other children and should be required to follow. They should not be given other work because children learn English by listening and watching. New English speakers appreciate avoidance of slang. "Stay on top of him" seems like a nonthreatening phrase, but when literally interpreted becomes quite a visual image.

Teachers must also be aware of the cultural customs of students new to the United States. Body language, conversational patterns, and social interactions are often very different from other students. A student who refuses to look a teacher in the eye or continually addresses the teacher as "Teacher" may be doing so out of respect rather than rudeness. Status designations based on age, sex, class, and occupation can alter relationships. Many cultures have differing concepts of cleanliness and emotions. Failure to recognize these differences can result in misinformation. Other students and staff members must be educated about the variety of culture expectations and beliefs that each student brings to school. The most important idea is to instill an attitude of respect and appreciation for the diversity that new cultures offer the school.

It is very difficult to determine whether an ESL student is experiencing academic difficulties as a result of language acquisition or a learning disability. Any student who is new to the United States should be given at least one year to adjust to the new educational system and to learn the language. However, when a student has been in the United States for several years and is still not learning at grade level, a special education referral may be necessary. Several questions must be asked. Are there any overt variables that immediately explain why the child is experiencing difficulties in the classroom? These variables may include family stressors, lack of experience, or lack of previous education. Significant behavioral concerns can also affect a student's ability to learn. Is the student proficient in his first language? If a student demonstrates learning concerns in both the first and second language, then a learning disability may be suspected. Are perceptual disorders noted? Children with learning disabilities have difficulties in the areas of visual perception, auditory perception, memory, attention, language, and motor integration. If a special education evaluation is required, it must be completed in both the native language and English. A comparison of the child's learning abilities in both languages is essential. Once the preferred language is determined, the intelligence assessment should be completed in the child's preferred language. A certified psychologist who is familiar with the child's cultural, linguistic, and educational background can ensure a nonbiased evaluation. If it is determined that the child has a learning disability, it is imperative that the classroom teacher, special educator, and ESL teacher work together to design an individual educational program to meet the very unique needs of this student.

Students who are learning English as a second language need many opportunities, both structured and in natural settings, to learn and use their new language. Classrooms that are language rich with cooperative learning activities lend themselves to English acquisition. Learning English as a second language is facilitated when language literacy is integrated throughout the curriculum and throughout all instructional activities. Meaningful interactions between students, and between the teacher and the student learning English, are more appropriate than rote drills and language rule memorization. The teaching of language expression should be integrated into each content area. As language acquisition becomes more fluid, students must be challenged toward higher levels of cognitive complexity.

## 7

# CHILDREN WITH
# ABOVE-AVERAGE ABILITIES

The day-to-day special educational needs of the gifted can be easily overlooked. Although it is apparent that children with less-than-average abilities need modification to their curriculum and assessment, the student with above-average abilities can "blend in with the crowd" and thereby not meet her full potential. Although gifted pull-out services are an excellent way to expand the curriculum for these students, it is imperative that their curriculum be modified continually and across curriculums. The general principles of adjusting the scope to each learner's ability apply to this group of students. In this case, instead of limiting the number and depth of core concepts to be mastered, the teacher must compact and also expand the curriculum.

In the "olden" days, when a teacher discovered that a student had above-average abilities, the teacher would give this student twice as many "dittos" to complete and then extra credit assignments to complete. If this talented student still had remaining time while the rest of the students completed work, this student would then be able to tutor lower-achieving students. It doesn't take long to see why these bright students soon wearied from the workload and expectations. Their above-average ability did not reap more exciting work, just more work! Today, we understand that gifted students need differentiation of instruction just as desperately as students with learning challenges. These students need to be challenged in order to preserve their thirst for knowledge. They must be challenged in exciting ways so that their intrinsic passion for learning will motivate them in future educational settings.

To meet that end, three principles apply for developing a curriculum for a gifted student. The first principle is to

*Dig a hole.*

To have a gifted child "dig a hole" means activities are created to help this child develop a deeper understanding of a concept. Although other students may be required to have a cursory understanding of the Civil Rights aspect of the Civil War, the gifted student may be asked to re-search the roots of the Civil Rights movement in Civil War actions. An-other principle is to have the student

*Build a bridge.*

Connection of current instruction to previous learning is a powerful method of instruction. The student must have a solid knowledge base of previous learning and then be able to relate current instruction to past experiences. This principle can also mean that through extensive learn-ing, a child may become curious as to the role a concept may have played in other situations. The gifted child would then be encouraged to connect current learning to future explorations. Using the Civil War ex-ample, the student might be curious as to racial views of people living in southern states today. Investigation in this area would build a bridge to future learning. The third principle of teaching gifted students is

*Make a tunnel.*

This principle encourages a student to research one small facet of in-struction. Young children usually do their first research project on a very general field, such as "dogs." As their learning styles and understanding of the concepts grows, they are able to limit their exploration to a small quadrant. Their next project might be limited to "working dogs." Finally, this same student might be inclined at a later date to investigate "the neurological makeup of working dogs vs. hunting dogs." Teacher guidance is necessary to help young gifted children limit the scope of their research. This is a developmental skill that initially requires teacher instruction. As the child develops interests in certain areas, the child is able to establish specific areas for continued learning.

There are two methods for delivering educational services to this population. In the pull-out model, a resource teacher takes the gifted student out of the classroom to work on projects involving higher-level thinking skills. These projects can include literature appreciation, advanced technology, science exploration, or mathematics acceleration. Each of these areas of instruction helps the gifted student to think in broader terms and develop a deeper understanding of academic concepts. But this delivery model alone is not enough. A gifted student's specialized educational needs cannot be met in a mere forty-minute period twice a week with a gifted teacher. As instruction must be differentiated throughout the day for the challenged learner, so must the educational program for the gifted student be differentiated to help these students meet their full potential. At times, utilizing the standard curriculum and methods of instruction may be appropriate, especially when a new concept is being introduced. The gifted student can participate in the introduction of new material and then be allowed to explore this material at a different level of understanding. At other times, if the gifted student has demonstrated a proficiency in the subject matter, an alternative assignment may best fit this student's needs.

A combination of pull-out instruction and extension of classroom work is essential. The expertise of the gifted teacher is essential to the classroom teacher when planning activities and lessons to meet these special needs. Coaching by gifted teachers is an excellent method to expand the classroom teacher's repertoire of teaching strategies. Part of every gifted teacher's schedule should be devoted to collaboration with the classroom teacher. This collaboration time can be devoted to monitoring the classroom needs of identified students, providing assistance with curriculum compacting and alternative assignments, and determining alternate methods of assessment.

The methods used for differentiating instruction for gifted students are the same as or similar to those methods used to alter instruction for any student. One method that works with a variety of students is curriculum compacting. After the teacher has taught a unit of study, the teacher is able to determine the core concepts that are essential to all students for future learning (see chapter 2). These core concepts then determine the goals of learning for each unit of study. If a gifted child has previously mastered these goals, then instruction is provided in complementary areas offering stimulating alternative assignments. A typical lament from gifted students is "I already know this!" Restudying material that has previously been mastered deteriorates motivation for continued learning. Allowing the gifted child to pursue other interests in the same venue peaks curiosity and inquisitive exploration.

Tiered assignments are a method applicable to all students utilizing differentiated instruction. The teacher develops a variety of levels of activities. Some students use repetition for learning while others use extension activities. A variety of resource materials is available for tasks that are adjusted by complexity, abstractness, concreteness, and level of independence. Some teachers who have taught a unit many times are able to develop tiered assessments utilizing different levels of questions according to Bloom's Taxonomy. Students are given what appear to be random tests although the teacher has adjusted each test for the level of learning of each student. Obviously, a teacher needs a high level of understanding of goals and content before developing such a complex method of assessment. This is perhaps the most extensive method of differentiation, one that requires an in-depth understanding of curriculum and goals, and a sincere dedication to differentiation.

Learning contracts are an excellent method of expanding the standard curriculum for gifted students (Tomlinson 1997; Winebrenner 1992). Students are given a pretest to determine the extent and depth of their understanding of a unit. The teacher and student determine what the child will do in place of the regular activity and develop a contract jointly. Included in the contract are working conditions, timelines, skills to be practiced and mastered, criteria for quality of work, assessment procedures, and positive and negative consequences for completed/uncompleted work. It is important to note that learning contracts, particularly for younger students, must be largely teacher directed. Younger students do not have the knowledge base to determine their own learning goals. The teacher is responsible for determining key concepts and structuring the activities for independent student work.

Study guides that outline major concepts for study can be developed for units. As the student and teacher review these study guides developed by the teacher, together they can decide upon alternative methods of studying key concepts. The gifted student can then use independent study to go into greater depth on a focused area of learning. These study guides can also be used to help students with learning challenges prepare for testing. Support staff members also appreciate having a condensed version of the unit of instruction.

Learning centers have been a tool for learning for many years. Areas containing a collection of activities and materials are set up around the classroom. These centers can be an excellent method for differentiating instruction. Some centers can be used by all students to teach, reinforce, or extend a skill (Kaplan, Kaplan, Madsen, and Gould 1980). These centers can offer a variety of activities that include simple to complex tasks. Some activities can be open-ended while others are highly structured. Other centers can be designed to meet the individual learning needs of specific students, such as the gifted student. In both cases, the learning center must be teacher-directed with clear directions and expectations. Activities should appeal to a variety of learning styles and interests. Learning centers also allow the teacher to have time to work with small groups of students while other students participate in the center activities.

Flexible grouping can allow for differentiation of instruction. Skill-based and interest-based groups can be created, either randomly or purposefully, to meet the needs of the students. This type of grouping allows for individualized instruction, either through extended exploration of topics or direct instruction and remediation. The determination of flexible grouping is based on a particular skill or unit of study rather than general learning abilities. Students must have opportunities to work with a variety of students, with time for both collaborative studying and independent work. Each of these methods of instruction can be seen in table 7.1. These methods work well with students of many different abilities. These strategies can be used to modify instruction for students with above-average abilities as well as for challenged learners.

**Table 7.1.  Differentiation Strategies**

| Method | Description | Considerations |
|---|---|---|
| Learning Centers | Stations throughout the room<br>Explore topics or practice skills<br>Variety of activities | All students don't do same tasks<br>Continually monitor student<br>  progress<br>Balance student choice and<br>  teacher choice<br>Can use centers heterogeneously<br>  or homogeneously<br>Balance between holding interest<br>  in topic and enough time to<br>  study in depth |
| Compacting | Assess what students currently know<br>Determine material to be mastered<br>Plan for learning new material<br>Excuse student from known material<br>Allows time for independent study | Why spend time "learning" what<br>  you already know?<br>Use written plan for learning<br>  and timelines<br>Helps eliminate boredom |
| Tiered Learning | Varied levels of activities<br>Builds on prior knowledge<br>Uses variety of methods of<br>  exploration | Use open-ended activities<br>Allows flexibility in learning<br>Helps with wide variety of<br>  learning abilities within a<br>  single lesson |
| Independent Study | Based on student interests and<br>  teacher facilitation<br>Mutual agreement on type of<br>  project | Can be productive for student<br>  with learning deficits<br>Can stimulate the difficult to<br>  motivate<br>Harvests curiosity<br>Teaches planning and research<br>  skills |
| Questioning | Teacher utilizes variety of levels of<br>  questions based on student needs<br>Literal levels of questions to students<br>  with special needs<br>High-level questions including utilizing<br>  higher-level thinking skills | Teach metacognition (awareness<br>  of one's thinking)<br>One lesson/many levels<br>Guaranteed right answer<br>Everyone a winner<br>Challenge students to reason |
| Contracts | Agreement between teacher and<br>  student<br>Certain freedoms granted in return<br>  for production of specific work | Motivational tool for special<br>  students<br>If used for one, should be offered<br>  to many<br>Can work with gifted or special<br>  needs student<br>Must establish clear expectations |
| Flexible Skills Grouping | Groups are determined by pretesting<br>  for specific skill mastery<br>Students can pass in and out of<br>  groups<br>No long-term grouping established | Students can advance at own pace<br>Allows for flexibility in learning<br>Should be mixed with<br>  heterogeneous grouping |

In addition, the standard curriculum can be expanded through the use of computers to create graphs, do presentations, or complete research. Drama, including plays, puppets, and audio performances, is an excellent alternate method of expressing ideas. Art can offer another avenue of expression for the gifted child. Writing, whether a song, story, poem, or journal, can allow flexibility in learning and assessment. Creativity can be expanded through the use of games, inventions, self-directed activities, and center composition.

When gifted students are given opportunities for differentiation, they are able to creatively meet their full potential and demonstrate their knowledge through alternative means. They are able to become self-motivated learners who enjoy the challenges of learning. Differentiation for these students is just as essential as for students with learning challenges.

# 8

# STUDENTS AT RISK
# OF SCHOOL FAILURE

Students who live in poverty, who live with only one parent, who have experienced a high rate of mobility and absenteeism, or who have had other instabilities within the home are considered at risk of school failure. These children have been affected by diverse economic, environmental, and geographic factors that have the potential to negatively impact their future learning. They are often unmotivated by the school curriculum, partly because of a lack of previous learning and often because of poor study skills, poor self-esteem, or a fear of failure. These students are not motivated to succeed using the standard curriculum when taught using "standard" methods. Their histories of previous academic failures make them cautious about taking risks as learners. Although these students do not qualify for special assistance under the auspices of special education, they are in need of changes in curriculum, changes in instruction, and changes in assessment to promote learning (Brown 1990).

Almost all children, regardless of their backgrounds, enter first grade full of enthusiasm about starting school. They are excited about the prospects of learning to read. Unfortunately, many of these students face academic failure at this young age that affects learning throughout the rest of their lives. During the beginning of their education, many students realize that they are not successful at learning. They see school as a threatening place that punishes students who do not do well. These students develop low self-esteem as a learner. A confident learner will take risks. If a confident learner doesn't understand a concept during instruction, the student will ask the teacher for clarification. The confident student expects herself to understand what is taught. A student who lacks self-esteem as a learner expects that she is incapable of understanding what is taught and therefore will not ask questions or seek assistance. When confronted with an opportunity to problem solve during an academic task, the student with low self-esteem will easily give up, without trying, for fear of failure. When this academic hopelessness is teamed with little support from home for academic success, these students appear destined for school failure. Therefore, it is imperative that schools intervene at a very early age to prevent the development poor self-concept as learner for these students. The teacher's responsibility is to build on the student's strengths, emphasizing small successes. All children must start out their school careers feeling successful and capable, with a confidence for attempting new areas of learning. Providing additional assistance to ensure a solid foundation of basic skills helps future learning. As discussed in chapter 2, it is important to always begin teaching a student at his level of success.

In order to build a student's confidence as a learner, the current level of functioning must be determined and instruction must begin at that level. The teacher and the student must set realistic goals that initially are easily attainable by the student. As the student's confidence as a learner improves and the repertoire of skills increases, tasks of a more advanced nature can be added gradually.

Just as students who are at risk of school failure are often not confident learners, they often do not see that they offer any personal significance as a person. Most typical learners feel secure in their position in the family and in the classroom. They know the areas in which they excel. They are proud of their accomplishments. In comparison, at-risk students have not had many opportunities for success. They do not have a strong sense of purpose or accomplishment in their lives. This also leads to a feeling of powerlessness over the direction of their lives. "Luck" is what will determine the future. When failure is met, the failure is a result of bad luck. Since luck is something that cannot be controlled, a need to improve skills is not felt. Schools can help students determine areas of interests and talent. When a student begins to feel success as a direct result of his efforts, the cycle of failure is broken.

Changes in the curriculum may be necessary to motivate at-risk students. Academic instruction must be teamed with real-world situations in order to make learning meaningful. Students need to understand the direct connection between learning geometry and how this skill will be used in later life. Without this connection, learning seems meaningless to this population. One method to team academics with real-world situations is to integrate academic and vocational skills. This is particularly useful for middle and high school students, who are more motivated if they see how a particular skill or activity will help them in the world of work. When interest in learning is raised, it is obvious that students are more likely to attend to task and persist in learning.

As in students with other learning challenges, students who are difficult to motivate also benefit from instruction in learning strategies and thinking skills. When taught effective methods of learning content, these students can become more successful in school. Skills of metacognition (planning, executing, and evaluating methods of learning) as well as cognitive learning strategies (note taking, test studying, time management) should be included in instruction (see chapter 5). Direct instruction in study skills is essential for this population. This instruction should include organizational techniques, note-taking skills, content reading, test-taking skills, memorization skills, and time management. Many commercial programs are available to teach these skills. Instruction in this area cannot be left to chance. It is a vital portion of the curriculum for students at risk of failure.

Lack of motivation is a concern with this population of students. It is difficult to instill a drive and desire for academic success. Helping a student to develop a sense of purpose and inspire initiative is a tough task. There are two ways to improve task completion and help to improve motivation for school assignments: reinforce completion of tasks with highly rewarding opportunities or punish by withdrawing positively reinforcing activities for the lack of completeness. When noncompletion of homework and class work becomes a schoolwide concern, a schoolwide program of reinforcement is effective. On Fridays for a half-hour period, students who complete assignments can be given opportunities to participate in creative activities such as cooking, sewing, listening to music, games, or free time. Each week, these activities can change based on student interests and staff and parent creativity. Parents can participate in this program by volunteering to teach sessions on their interests such as painting, photography, woodworking, magic tricks, or collection displays. Each week, students can choose between different activities if work is completed. Those students who do not complete their assignments must spend the time in a study hall. It is imperative that the weekly sessions are rewarding for students. Many creative, free or inexpensive, and easy activities can be designed by and for the students. Older students enjoy creating opportunities for younger children or their peers. Sometimes the most appreciated activity is simply time to relax with friends. All students can benefit from such a program but especially students at risk of failure.

The other method that should be balanced with reinforcing strategies is consequences for noncompliance. Homework and class work should not be considered an option but a requirement. Beginning with primary grades, the school must stress to students and parents that work completion is not an option. All efforts should be made to assist the student with work completion during the school day. After-school study halls, opportunities for lunch study halls, or individual help from the teacher are positive methods of assisting the student. If a student refuses to complete work during the school day or for homework when necessary, consequences should be given in a tiered system. Beginning violations warrant a note or phone call home to advise parents of impending problems. Cooperation from parents is enlisted. Repeated offenses result in required study halls after school. Continued refusal to complete work demands later study halls into evening hours or Saturday detention. Homework completion should initially be given as much positive assistance as possible to help the student begin to develop intrinsic rewards for work done well. Extrinsic motivators may need to be given in the beginning to assist in this process. If positive reinforcement is unsuccessful, then consequences should be teamed with plenty of positive reinforcement for work completed under any circumstance.

School climate has been found to have a strong effect on student learning, especially for those students who are difficult to motivate (Hill,

Foster, and Gendler 1990). When schools are sensitive to the responsibilities and outside problems of the students, students feel more support. Schools that embrace diversity and respect students, regardless of their economic or culture background, allow students to learn with pride. Students who are dealing with tremendous outside stressors such as hunger or domestic violence may need adaptations made to homework assignments. Homeless students who face an array of outside concerns need to have their primary needs met (food, shelter, safety) before educational needs can be met. Often, schools must provide assistance in meeting families' basic needs so that higher levels of needs can be met. Directing families to outside agencies becomes the responsibility of the schools. Environmentally challenged students need to feel acceptance and concern from school officials.

Flaxman, Ascher, and Harrington (1988) found that students who have caring adults who serve as their mentors or advocates are more successful in school. Teachers and other school personnel who serve in this role develop a one-to-one relationship with a student, providing support and intervening on the student's behalf as needed. One effective method for middle and high school students is to provide a caring school figure by establishing a homeroom period used specifically for the purpose of discussing issues such as character, career, and school topics (Maeroff 1990). Engaging students in conversation dealing with nonschool issues can help open the lines of communication (Farner 1996). Having a positive role model who shows genuine concern for a student can offer the motivation to succeed in school.

The more parents participate in school in a sustained way, the better for student achievement (Gordon 1978). The importance of parent participation is undisputed. The difficulty lies in the methodology for involving parents where poverty exists, long hours at a job are necessary, and family struggles are prevalent. When parents have had negative experiences in school as students, their motivation to participate in the education of their children is minimal. Schools must develop creative methods to encourage parent participation. In order to generate better communication between schools and parents, schools must be sensitive to parents' scheduling difficulties and consider work schedules when determining parent/teacher conferences and curriculum nights. Nontraditional parents, such as grandparents serving in parental roles, single parents, divorced parents, and parents with joint custody, must be welcomed at school events. Every attempt should be made to make the first contact with a parent a positive one. Mailing home positive notes regarding student achievement or leaving a positive message on an answering machine can help parents to not dread phone calls from school. Parents of students at risk of failure have often been beleaguered with negative phone calls from school. The surprise of a positive call may help clear previously negative feelings regarding school. Most parents are anxious to help their children succeed but are often untrained and do not know how to assist. Epstein (1984) found that when teachers help parents of students considered at risk, those students can be as effective as those with parents who have more education.

Children who are considered at risk of school failure have many outside problems that interfere with learning. In addition, some schools appear to devalue their talents and potential in light of their frequent failures. Although these students are in dire need of curricular and instructional modifications and assistance, they are not covered by special education regulations. Schools and teachers must foster resiliency in these children by building on their strengths. Resiliency is the ability to adapt and succeed despite risk and adversity. Students who are facing constant outside challenges, in particular, must be taught social competence, problem-solving skills, autonomy, and a sense of purpose and future (Bernard 1995). Instruction must connect with the student's culture and prior knowledge while being directly linked to future opportunities and the world of work. Engaged learning opportunities encourage students to become active learners who participate and take responsibility for their education. Although the mastery of basic skills is of primary importance, students at risk need an academically challenging curriculum that uses higher-level thinking skills rather than merely rote memory. Finally, families and schools need to work together to teach and nurture children. When families are involved with the school to improve the student's self-esteem, to value the educational program, and to insist on academic success, the at-risk cycle can be broken.

# 9

# CLASSROOM MANAGEMENT

**E**ffective teaching necessitates managing myriad tasks simultaneously. This is true in any classroom, but particularly true in differentiated classrooms. Consistency, structure, and fairness are requirements to ensure that a classroom flows smoothly. Discipline must be based on mutual respect and a sense of belonging. Students should be allowed to help make decisions about classroom management, understanding that there are natural and logical consequences for all actions. The goal of any classroom management program is to teach self-discipline.

Five common elements exist in classrooms with strong behavioral management programs (Swift and Spivack 1975). First, a one-to-one relationship is developed between the teacher and each child. The teacher relates to each child on a personal level, establishing rapport and getting to know each child on an individual basis. Second, the teacher acts as a model, talking out classroom problems with students and modeling appropriate methods of dealing with frustration. The third commonality is a positive classroom environment where a child can anticipate positive reactions and a nonjudgmental attitude from the teacher. Children are encouraged through recognition, even if only partial achievement is met. The child is encouraged to share ideas and opinions, and opinions are accepted even if these opinions don't change the situation. Fourth, environmental demands are clarified with preestablished rules of acceptable behavior. Careful specification of directions, goals, and actions are explained. Students are quickly informed when behavior is becoming inappropriate, what will happen as a result of inappropriate behavior, and feedback about the effectiveness of behavior. Finally, these effective teachers foster self-control and independent problem solving. Students are helped to generate and verbalize their own thoughts and expressions, determine their own methods of self-monitoring behavior, and become involved in decision making. A classroom is created where the tolerance of personal opinions is demanded and risk taking as a learner is encouraged. Through this system, a student gains confidence in himself and becomes more self-disciplined and self-motivated.

What is your teaching style? Complete the survey in table 9.1, selecting either A or B, whichever most closely describes your style. There are no correct answers and no answers are better than others. This is an informal inventory to determine how you feel the most comfortable in the classroom. After completing the survey, use the scoring key to decide whether you enjoy an unstructured setting or a structured classroom. Either classroom can work for many students; however, a structured classroom where students can predict events and consequences generally works best when differentiated instruction is used. Every classroom has a need to be unstructured at times, as long as set guidelines for behavior have been established and followed. In a teacher-directed classroom, the teacher determines instruction and strategies to learn the curriculum as well as the rules and procedures. In a student-directed classroom, the teacher and the students jointly determine rules and procedures. Obviously, the teacher must decide curriculum, but the students are encouraged to be active participants in the learning process. In any type of classroom, it is imperative that a positive relationship exist between the teacher and the student. In a high school setting, where teachers deal with many students on a daily basis, this relationship is certainly more difficult to build. Some attempt must be made by the teacher in this situation to glean some personal knowledge of each student to avoid "production-line" teaching, in which students become numbers rather than individuals.

In a democratic classroom, structure and order are evident. Students know what is expected of them, both behaviorally and academically, and

**Table 9.1. Determine Your Teaching Style**

Select either A or B, whichever more closely describes how you feel:

1. A. I feel most comfortable when I complete weekly lesson plans.
   B. I prefer to teach spontaneously rather than planning ahead.
2. A. I make lists.
   B. Planning ahead is not a priority for me.
3. A. My classroom is basically student directed/teacher planned.
   B. My classroom is teacher directed/student planned.
4. A. I determine my classroom rules at the beginning of the year.
   B. Students determine rules at the beginning of the year with my input.
5. A. The good of the group outweighs the individual.
   B. I try to spend time alone with each student on a regular basis.
6. A. I know many facts about my students' personal lives.
   B. I prefer to concentrate on classroom concerns.
7. A. I am firm but fair in determining consequences.
   B. Students determine consequences for negative behavior.
8. A. My role is to be the students' leader.
   B. My role is to be the students' model.
9. A. Rules may be affected by outside influences.
   B. Rules are made to be followed.
10. A. In the trunk of my car are emergency supplies.
    B. I can list the contents of my car trunk.
11. A. I work best under the pressure of a deadline.
    B. I like to have holiday shopping completed well in advance.
12. A. I prefer heterogeneous classroom grouping.
    B. I prefer homogeneous classroom grouping.
13. A. I enjoy a noisy classroom.
    B. I prefer a busy classroom under noise control.

## SCORING KEY

Circle the numbers below if you circled them on the survey. Add the total circled in each column to determine your teaching style.

| Structured: | Unstructured | Student-Directed | Teacher-Directed |
|---|---|---|---|
| 1A | 1B | 3A | 3B |
| 2A | 2B | 4B | 4A |
| 10A | 10B | 7B | 7A |
| 11A | 11B | 8B | 8A |
| 12B | 12A | | |
| 13B | 13A | | |

| Relationship with Student | Little Relationship with Student |
|---|---|
| 5B | 5A |
| 6A | 6B |
| 9A | 9B |

understand the consequences of compliance and of noncompliance with classroom rules. Students are active partners in the development of a management plan based on mutual trust. An atmosphere is established of caring for one another, stressing cooperation more than competition. Students and teacher are aware that the behavior management plan may need to be altered based on situations and student/teacher needs.

A well-developed plan of classroom management includes three phases of discipline (Nagy 1988): prevention, reactive discipline, and a success system. A good system of prevention includes managerial techniques of movement, transitions, alertness, variety, and "withitness." An optimal lesson demonstrating effective teacher movement has few times of off-task behavior by the teacher (such as nagging, preaching, or moralizing). During teaching time, little time should be spent telling children what to do (such as "Sit up straight"). Instead, nonverbal reminders to return to task or follow along with teacher directions are more effective methods of maintaining lesson flow. A teacher who demonstrates poor transition or "jerkiness" switches activities quickly, usually due to lack of teacher planning. In comparison, a teacher who offers smooth transitions gives students warning of changes in instruction. Materials are readily available to begin instruction immediately. Classrooms with alertness and accountability are filled with unpredictable excitement. These teachers begin instruction with "You'll never believe what happens in this story. Read to find out." Students are challenged to learn new concepts and praised for their attempts. The teacher circulates throughout the room, ensuring that every student receives the necessary attention. A variety of props and teaching techniques is used to keep interest high. Accountability or "withitness" is demonstrated because the teacher is aware of who is behaving and who needs additional assistance to remain on task. The teacher is able to stop major disruptions promptly while ignoring minor concerns. Accountability includes the ability to manage overlapping activities, ensuring an awareness of all that is occurring in the classroom.

A "ripple effect" occurs in a well-constructed classroom. The teacher is strong and positive, disciplining students with firmness and follow through as needed. Clarity is offered by telling a student exactly what behavior is unacceptable, using a firm voice and actions that demonstrate willingness to follow through on teacher directions. As a result, this firm and clear discipline has a ripple effect, from the offender to every other student in the class. An excellent technique for improving overall class behavior is described by Nagy as "deviant prestige." If a teacher can get the child with the worst behavior problem on her side, the rest of the class will follow. It pays to spend additional time making a positive relationship with the most disruptive student in order to have classroom compliance by others.

Carl Rogers (1969) is perhaps the most popular proponent of the humanistic movement, or the need to consider a child's inner needs. He believed that students have a natural desire to learn that can be expanded in an environment with a positive relationship with adults built on trust. The components of such a classroom include a genuine concern by the teacher for each child, in an atmosphere of acceptance and nonjudgment. The teacher focuses on the construction side of behavior, reminding students of all of their successes, while disciplining inappropriate behavior. This helps the child to move forward constructively. The child has the responsibility to make decisions, while finding solutions and taking risks in a nonthreatening environment. The teacher guides children in decision making while children are able to become less defensive and more open to taking risks.

---

Rule #10
Develop a relationship.

---

Before any behavior management plan can be enacted, a positive relationship must be established between the student and the teacher. This can be accomplished when the teacher offers encouragement, understanding, and acceptance of a student's feelings, expecting the best achievement and behavior. Teachers can help establish relationships with students by helping students label and interpret problems. Teachers should be careful of advising, judging, or criticizing a child's attempt at problem solving; instead, teachers should listen carefully to the child's statements and mirror the child's feelings and perceptions. A highly effective method of developing a positive relationship with a student is to use the "helper principle." Helping others is a wonderful method of building self-esteem and confidence. In addition, when a student is placed in a helping role, opportunities for praise are abundant. A teacher has many tasks that need completion throughout the school day. Assigning "important" tasks, especially those that require teacher trust to be completed, and praising the completion of such tasks establishes a positive relationship. Once this positive relationship has been developed, behavioral interventions are more effective because these interventions are based on trust and concern rather than anger or belittling.

External conditions that affect behavior can be controlled through the use of applied behavioral analysis. B. F. Skinner (1982) is the leader of the behaviorist movement that believed all behavior could be explained by a response to environmental stimuli. If a behavior increases, it has a history of being reinforced. If a child is motivated, it is because he has learned to associate certain behaviors with certain outcomes. Reinforcers can be either positive or negative. If the reinforcer increases behavior, then it is positive. Three types of positive reinforcers can be used. A primary reinforcer is a tangible item, such as food, that is offered for a desired behavior. A social reinforcer is attention or praise. A token reinforcer has value when it is exchanged for a reinforcing item or event. Although primary reinforcers are highly motivating for very young children or students with severe disabilities, teachers should work to use social, token, or delayed reinforcers that lead to events rather than tangible items. It is difficult to stimulate self-discipline when students are continually reinforced for expected behaviors using tangible reinforcers. Children become dependent on outside "gifts" to completed work. Instead, token reinforcers that can lead to additional recess or lessened homework are more effective in developing self-motivation and discipline. A success system allows students to have clear, fair expectations with appropriate reinforcements and consequences. Situations are set up so that students can succeed. Students know exactly what is expected of them, and they know exactly what will happen when they meet these expectations or fail to meet these expectations.

Punishment decreases behavior, but it does not replace the inappropriate behavior with an appropriate behavior. Punishment often works in the short term, but does little to assist in long-term goals for self-discipline.

When a teacher screams at a student for inappropriate behavior, the behavior will generally stop but will often reoccur. If punishment is used, it must be teamed with the immediate positive reinforcement of desired behaviors. Whenever a student is told what not to do, the student must be praised when any attempt is made for appropriate behavior. This is a difficult task for teachers when the highly disruptive student is continually gaining attention from the teacher and students for inappropriate behavior. It may appear that the student is misbehaving in order to "get the teacher's goat." The teacher must remain professional and reinforce any attempt that the disruptive student makes at work completion and appropriate behavior.

Occasionally, time-out procedures can be effective in altering negative behavior. Removing a student from the social setting can allow both the teacher and the student an opportunity to reevaluate the situation. However, continually sending a student to the office or into the hall can eventually become a reinforcer, allowing the student to leave undesirable learning tasks. Brief periods of time-out, especially with young children, can be a highly effective method of behavior management.

A highly effective method of altering behavior is shaping. Small steps towards the eventual goals are reinforced. Students can take a very long time to totally change their behaviors or learning abilities. Through shaping, small attempts and successes at meeting the ultimate goal are positive reinforced, leading to more small attempts at completion. A student may be unable to complete an entire homework assignment accurately in a reasonable amount of time. The teacher might begin by assigning half of the assignment and expecting a high level of accuracy. Gradually, the number of problems will be expanded, reinforcing the child for each incremental step. It is important to reinforce these small steps so that a student does not become frustrated at the length of time required to totally change a behavior or learn a new concept. In addition, shaping helps the teacher recognize the progress being made.

Finally, some theorists believe that students develop as a result of the interaction between their inner needs and outer forces. One of the most prominent theorists of this belief was Rudolf Driekurs (1968). Driekurs believed that all behavior is purposeful, directed toward achieving social recognition or belonging to a group. The teacher's role is to help the student recognize the purpose of the behavior and change that behavior into a more appropriate method of achieving the goal. Driekurs believes that a child misbehaves for only four reasons: getting attention, in a contest for power seeking revenge, or displaying inadequacy.

A child seeking attention can achieve this goal by two methods. A "constructive" method is the child who reminds peers and teacher what a good student should do (sometimes called "The Eddie Haskel Syndrome" after the *Leave It to Beaver* character who forever brown-nosed adults) and who requires incessant praise. This child often has not had to share the spotlight with others and finds it difficult to let other students shine. A student who demonstrates the "destructive" method of attention getting practices what Burton White (1995) calls the "Saga of the Soggy Potato Chip." No one likes soggy potato chips, but when starving on a desert island, a soggy potato chip could be quite satisfying. When a child does not receive praise for positive actions, the child will resort to negative behavior in order to gain recognition from the teacher and peers. It is the teacher's responsibility to find positive methods of reinforcing any attempts at appropriate behavior. Typically, these students do not receive positive attention at home and need additional reinforcement from teachers to fill this need.

Second, student misbehavior can take the form of a contest for power. A child who has grown up in an environment of criticism and pressure will develop the need to enter into a power struggle with authority figures. A teacher must remove herself from the contest by quietly insisting that teacher directions be completed, while allowing the student as much influence upon the decision as possible. Using a choice of two options determined by the teacher can often be effective.

A child who seeks revenge against other students, staff, or animals feels that he is unable to gain attention or power. This is the student who hurts other students or a class pet and does not feel remorse. This student feels that people are the cause of pain and should be treated with maliciousness and humiliation. The classroom teacher must immediately contact the social worker or psychologist for assistance. These students can grow up to have significant societal problems.

Finally, some students resort to helplessness or inadequacy to meet their needs. This child has given up on the possibility of meeting goals independently. Learned helplessness results because the child has learned that by feigning helplessness, other people will complete tasks and meet needs. This is generally a result of experiencing many failures and seeing no hope for success.

How is a teacher to react to each of these needs? First, the teacher should observe the child in a variety of settings to determine if the need expressed by the behavior is unique to the teacher's classroom or expressed throughout the day. If the inappropriate behavior occurs only in the classroom, then perhaps the teacher needs to reevaluate whether the child is given enough positive reinforcement for appropriate behavior, or if the child is placed in a power struggle. If the behavior occurs across settings, then the teacher must determine the purpose of the child's behavior. The purpose can often be identified by the spontaneous reaction of the teacher. The automatic response of the teacher is usually what the child wants the teacher to feel, whether it be attention, revenge, power struggle, or helplessness. Next, the teacher can observe the child's response to teacher correction. If a child is attempting to put on a coat and is having problems, the child wanting attention will be glad for help and will respond excitedly. The child who is in a contest for power will turn to another activity and refuse to put on the coat. The child seeking revenge will physically hurt the teacher offering assistance. The child demonstrating inadequacy will passively allow the teacher to put on the coat. The best rule is not to do what the child expects. The teacher should not follow this first impulse. Generally, it is best to do the opposite of first impulse, especially when unsure of the goal of the behavior. In table 9.2, the goal indicated by each behavior is shown as well as procedures to be used to remediate inappropriate behavior.

After hypothesizing about the student's goal for misbehaving, the teacher should discuss the purpose behind the inappropriate behavior with the student in a private setting. This meeting should not occur immediately after the misbehavior but rather at a time when both the teacher and student can remain unemotional and factual. If the teacher correctly identifies the purpose for the behavior, a recognition reflex will occur such as nervous smiling, lack of eye contact, or signs of response. This indicates that the teacher has correctly identified the goal. Once the goal of the behavior has been identified, the teacher and the student should discuss appropriate methods of achieving this goal. Once again, all small attempts by the student at remediating his inappropriate behavior should be recognized and reinforced.

**Table 9.2.    How to Correct Behavior**

| Goal of Behavior | Initial Reaction | Corrective Procedure |
|---|---|---|
| Attention | Annoyed feeling<br>Pleased with "good" child<br>Frustration with demanding<br>  behavior | Ignore attention-seeking<br>  behavior<br>Give attention when child<br>  is not seeking it<br>Do not show annoyance |
| Power | Provoked<br>Ready to fight<br>Threatened | Don't fight<br>Don't give in<br>Avoid power struggles<br>Give two choices |
| Revenge | Hurt<br>Mad<br>Outrage | IMMEDIATELY SEEK<br>    PROFESSIONAL HELP |
| Display Inadequacy | Despair<br>Frustration | Stop all criticism<br>Praise all attempts<br>Use chaining<br>Build confidence |

Another very popular method of classroom management is discussed in *Assertive Discipline,* written by Lee and Marlene Canter in 1976. This discipline system is based on the premise that the teacher has the right to teach, and students have the right to learn. Teachers using this approach have an established discipline plan with rules and consequences. The teacher follows through with this discipline plan in an assertive but nonhostile approach. An assertive teacher makes sure that teacher directions are followed without aggressive or hostile means. A hostile teacher responds to students in negative, sarcastic, or degrading terms, abusing the child's rights and feelings. An assertive teacher gives positive recognition to good behavior while clearly communicating expectations and consequences.

When an inappropriate behavior has occurred, the assertive teacher approaches the child using a composed voice while making direct eye contact. Using the child's name, the teacher tells the student what behavior should be occurring at that time (e.g., "Your eyes belong on the board.") The student is given a choice of two acceptable choices while the teacher employs the "broken record technique" of repeating instructions quietly and not allowing excuses. An example of a hostile approach to discipline  is when the teacher berates a student as a method of disciplining; the goal is for the teacher to "win" the battle. Table 9.3

**Table 9.3. Hostile/Assertive Approach to Discipline**

*Hostile Approach to Discipline*

| | |
|---|---|
| Teacher: | Matt, I'm not going to put up with your refusing to do your work. You will do your work in this class. |
| Student: | I don't give a darn what you say. |
| Teacher: | Don't you talk to me that way. Who do you think you are? |
| Student: | Who do you think you are? |
| Teacher: | Listen, young man. I'm not going to take this from you. |
| Student: | (sticks out tongue) |
| Teacher: | You are disgusting. You'll be sorry for what you are saying. I won't tolerate children talking to me this way. Get out of here! |

*Assertive Approach to Discipline*

| | |
|---|---|
| Teacher: | Matt, I want to talk to you. Please sit down. |
| Student: | Why? I didn't do nothing! |
| Teacher: | (looking him in the eye) Matt, you can no longer disrupt the class. You will do your work. |
| Student: | You always pick on me. |
| Teacher: | (repeating) Matt, you will do your work when I tell you to. |
| Student: | OK. I know you mean it. |
| Teacher: | Yes, Matt, and if you choose to disrupt and not do your work, you will be kept after for detention. |
| Student: | It's hard for me to do the work. |
| Teacher: | I understand. I'll be there to help if you need it. Now I want to make sure you understand. Please repeat the rules to me. |

shows this hostile approach as well as the assertive approach where the teacher lets the student know the rules while allowing the student to maintain dignity. Use of the assertive discipline model ensures that students can change their behavior without fear of humiliation. The teacher and the student are both winners.

Finally, student contracts can be an excellent method of classroom management. A student, or students, and the teacher jointly determine tasks to be included in a written contract. The tasks may be academic or behavioral in nature and may include homework completion, appropriate behavior, or improvement of academic skills. Privileges and rewards are determined jointly by the student and the teacher, as are the consequences for a broken contract. The criteria for mastery are agreed, and a formal contract is written. It is imperative that the contract be in writing to ensure agreement by all parties. Model contracts are shown in table 9.4.

**Table 9.4.    Sample Behavior Contracts**

CONTRACT

This contract is between _____ and _____.

As the student, I agree to:

1. Stop before I call out to the teacher for help.
2. Use at least one other source for help before I ask the teacher, like my book, a friend, my notes.
3. To check off on my "Help" sheet which kind of help I have tried to use.

As the teacher, I agree to:

1. Give five bonus points for each period/assignment during which this procedure is followed.

_____          _____
Student                                                      Teacher


CONTRACT

STUDENT:    I agree to look at my teacher when she is talking.
                   I agree not to talk while my teacher is talking.
TEACHER:    I agree to call Al by name when giving instructions.
                   I agree to give Al a check for each time he follows this agreement.
PRINCIPAL: I agree to meet with Al every Friday to see how he is doing.
PARENT:      I agree to let Al choose dessert on Fridays if he has earned 10 checks during the week.


SIGNED: _____    _____

            _____    _____


**Table 9.5.    Proactive vs. Reactive Strategies**

| Strategy | Proactive | Reactive |
|---|:---:|:---:|
| Build a positive relationship | X | |
| Positive reinforcement of appropriate behavior | X | |
| Structured expectations | X | |
| Organized, active lessons | X | |
| Democratic classroom | X | |
| Social skills training of character education and emotional intelligence | X | |
| Student/teacher contracts | X | X |
| Assertive discipline | | X |
| Confronting behavior | | X |
| Punishment/response cost | | X |
| Logical consequences | | X |
| Student choice of teacher options | X | X |

Classroom management is difficult for any teacher. It is particularly challenging for teachers who practice differentiated instruction. So many activities, so many levels of learning, so many types of learning are going on simultaneously that a teacher must have "eyes in the back of her head" to keep the classroom on an even keel. By reviewing the strategies listed in table 9.5, teachers can work on using proactive strategies whenever possible and saving reactive strategies for those times when nothing else is effective.

# 10

# BRINGING THE STAFF TOGETHER

The most important component of differentiated instruction in a school is helping the staff become united. Teachers and support staff must work together for the benefit of each child in order for differentiated instruction to occur throughout the school day and throughout a student's education. Everyone within the school building must be dedicated to the individual needs of each student. To develop cohesive teams, members need to have a commitment to differentiated instruction, accountability to the student and the organization, and the skills necessary to develop and implement an effective program. When each member of the educational team is interdependent upon other members of the team to ensure a successful program for each child, then true teaming exists. Staff members do not need to socialize outside of school to develop this camaraderie, but they need to be dedicated to a meaningful purpose, specific goals, and a common approach for which they hold themselves mutually accountable (Katzenbach and Smith 1993). Working together for a common purpose creates a synergy in which the whole is greater than the sum of its parts.

To build effective educational teams, the school climate must embrace an environment that fosters teamwork. Class schedules must allow time for collaboration between teachers on a regularly scheduled basis. Opportunities for joint planning, problem solving, and curriculum expansion must be scheduled frequently. Teachers no longer work in the isolation of their classrooms, but rather in concert with many professionals throughout the day.

In addition, a climate of mutual respect for each member of the team must be established. The first step in developing respect for each other is to discuss professional values and goals. The following are some helpful exercises to be completed by all staff members, including teachers, aides, administrators, secretaries, social workers, psychologist, nurse, and others. One person needs to act as the facilitator to help team members complete each exercise and share insights, if they feel comfortable. The purpose of the activities is to help team members determine their own strengths and weaknesses as team members and to see the strengths of others. In table 10.1, team members should take time to reflect on their personal values, goals, and attributes. The professional goals are then used with table 10.2, where staff members determine their two most important goals and share these goals with team members. Team members then help each other decide which qualities and strengths each possesses that will enable them to achieve their goals. This exercise is a wonderful team-building session, stressing the positive attributes of each team member. Table 10.3 is then used for team members to rank job qualities that are important to them. These are shared with team members so that each person can understand what qualities other team members are seeking from their jobs.

These activities will help each staff member to thoughtfully consider his professional needs, goals, and personality type. By discussing these factors as a team, each member will begin to better understand herself and other team members. These questions were developed to be nonthreatening for group discussion and to facilitate the concept that teams need a variety of personalities to be effective. The questions and activities also begin to foster a "group" mentality rather than

**Table 10.1.   Who Am I?**

| |
|---|
| What are the five most important values to me? |
| What are my professional goals? |
| What are my attributes? |

**Table 10.2.   Helping Hand**

Outline your hand on a piece of paper.

Write down your two most important professional goals.

Share those goals with your team.

As each person shares his or her goals, decide which qualities or strengths you think this person possesses that will help meet these goals.

Circulate around the table and list one quality on each person's hand.

**Table 10.3.   What's Important to You?**

Rate in order of importance to you, 8 being highest.
Share your responses with your team.

| Job Attribute | Rating (1–8) |
| --- | --- |
| Autonomy | |
| Professional Support | |
| Emotional Support | |
| Opportunities for Creativity | |
| Leadership Opportunities | |
| Recognition | |
| Intellectual Stimulation | |
| Social Involvement | |

"individual" mentality. Individual differences can be celebrated as necessary components of effective teams. Effective teams have a mix of people who contribute in different but complementary ways.

As team members become more cognizant of each other's personalities and professional needs, each member must also understand what he brings to the team composition. Certain responsibilities are required for teams to work in unity. Daniel Goleman (1995), in his book *Emotional Intelligence,* discusses how individuals can learn to manage emotions and recognize emotions in others. A simple inventory based on Goleman's work can be used to help staff members begin to realize their strengths and weaknesses as team members. As each team member completes table 10.4, they are able to begin recognizing their personal strengths and weaknesses regarding their emotions. After reflecting upon this exercise, members are able to complete table 10.5, which pinpoints emotional areas for improvement. This exercise is not to be shared with team members but rather used for personal reflection. Table 10.6 is then used for group discussion. The group facilitator goes through each area of emotional intelligence.

Discussion can then follow about how the synergy of the team can be enhanced; what can each member of the team do individually to help the overall effectiveness of the combined members?

When team members take a hard look at their own strengths and weaknesses as individual team members, they become more accepting of other team members' flaws. In addition, team members begin to consider how their emotions affect others. It is important that these activities take place at the beginning of the school year, when teams are beginning to form and before negative teams have had opportunities to be established.

Negative teams can be characterized by five traits: dramatic, suspicious, detached, depressed, or compulsive (Aubrey and Felkins 1988). Dramatic teams have a strong leader who is idealized by others. This leader keeps everyone motivated. These teams generally dissolve when the strong leader leaves the team, because there hasn't been a sharing of leadership. Everyone on a team needs to be empowered in order to ensure an effective team.

In a suspicious team, a lack of trust is evident between members. Members often intimidate each other as they jockey for power. They are reactive in their purpose, rather than proactively developing methodology for children.

**Table 10.4. Emotional Intelligence Quiz**
**[based on Goleman (1995)]**

| Answer each question either true or false. | T/F |
|---|---|

1. I can recognize when I am angry and at whom I am angry.
2. I vent my anger in nondestructive ways.
3. I generally consider the consequences of my words and actions before speaking or acting.
4. I exercise regularly.
5. I engage in a relaxing activity daily.
6. I enjoy being with people of different viewpoints and backgrounds.
7. I am able to take another person's perspective and understand their feelings.
8. When other people talk, I listen without thinking about what I will say next.
9. I am able to distinguish between what someone does or says and my own reactions or judgment to it.
10. I know how to send "I" messages.
11. I understand and practice "reflective listening."
12. I am able to disclose my feelings to others whom I trust.
13. I value openness in others.
14. I am able to identify patterns in my emotional life (e.g., how I handle anger, when I get depressed, and how I can release stress).
15. I see myself in a positive light.
16. I can recognize my own strengths and weaknesses.
17. I am able to laugh at myself.
18. I take responsibility for my actions.
19. I am not a victim.
20. I know when to lead and when to follow.
21. I can state my concerns and feelings without anger or passivity.
22. I fight fairly.
23. I utilize the "win/win" model of negotiations.
24. I look for compromises.
25. I consider myself a good team player.

A detached team lacks warmth and emotion. In the dramatic team, there is only one leader. In the detached team, there is no leader. Leadership is a role that is to be shared among every member of the team depending on the situation. In a detached team, it appears that no member cares enough to offer leadership at any time.

A depressed team lacks initiative and motivation. There is no sense of direction. Because of past failures, this team is afraid to take risks. Members consider current, ineffective practices to be better than attempting new strategies that could fail.

Finally, a compulsive team is rigid, lacking creativity and initiative. Team members are attached to tradition and are often heard saying, "We've always done it this way." These teams members are unwilling to put forth the effort needed to become creative and enthusiastic.

**Table 10.5.    Emotional Intelligence Thoughts**
**[based on Daniel Goleman]**

DO YOU:

KNOW YOUR EMOTIONS?
Do you have a well-developed self-awareness of the emotions you display?

MANAGE YOUR EMOTIONS?
Are you able to shake off anxiety, bounce back quickly after minor disappointments, avoid a doom-and-gloom attitude?

MOTIVATE YOURSELF?
Can you delay gratification and impulsiveness to achieve a higher level?

RECOGNIZE EMOTIONS IN OTHERS?
Are you attuned to subtle signs of other peoples' emotions?

HANDLE RELATIONSHIPS WELL?
Do you demonstrate effective social competence?

Honestly consider each of these questions to determine your personal strengths and weaknesses as a team member.

How can negative teams be improved? The first step is to identify and combat unnecessary rules and procedures. Honest discussion on "why" strategies are used must be completed, often against the resistance of team members. Abuses of power must be challenged and new opportunities for shared leadership developed. Team members need to critically evaluate past and present strategies and power distribution while initiating and reinforcing creativity. This process can often be painful and detrimental to current teams. Often, new teams need to be formed when negative teams have been in existence for extended periods of time.

In comparison, effective teams agree on clear and challenging goals. Many different teams exist within one school. Each of these teams may

**Table 10.6. How to Improve Your Emotional Intelligence [based on Goleman (1995)]**

| | Area for Improvement? |
|---|---|
| **UNDERSTAND YOURSELF**<br>• Develop a self-awareness of feelings and how to deal with them.<br>• Improve your emotional self-control. | |
| **MANAGE YOUR EMOTIONS**<br>• Develop a balance of accepting emotions and shrugging off emotions.<br>• Deal with anger immediately. Diffuse and challenge thoughts that trigger it. Cool down until adrenal surge doesn't trigger more. Calm down before venting. | |
| **ANXIETY**<br>• Remember that worrying begets worrying.<br>• Stop worrisome thoughts at the beginning.<br>• Try distractions when worry is unpreventable. | |
| **IMPROVE YOUR ATTITUDE**<br>• Work on your motivation, your zeal for life, your persistence.<br>• Control your foul moods.<br>• Utilize positive thinking and optimism. | |
| **BE EMPATHETIC**<br>• Try seeing the world through someone else's prospective.<br>• Let your thoughts center on someone else rather than you. | |
| **IMPROVE YOUR INTERPERSONAL SKILLS**<br>• Change your role in groups (from leader to follower).<br>• Negotiate solutions.<br>• First listen, then speak. | |
| **UNDERSTAND YOUR OWN NEEDS**<br>• Determine how you can fulfill your own needs.<br>• Develop good life skills (exercise/eating/socializing/relaxing). | |
| **IMPROVE YOUR TEAMING SKILLS**<br>• Maximize other peoples' talents.<br>• Promote cooperation.<br>• Take initiative and be willing to do some "grunt work." | |

have different specific goals but must share a common purpose or philosophy regarding the mission of the school. Grade-level goals may focus on specific curricular and developmental goals while school-based teams may focus on social and academic goals for the learning community. When a team of teachers shares the same vision that all students need to be educated to the fullest extent and that this vision requires differentiated instruction by all staff members, a quality educational program can be developed from preschool through high school graduation. Each teacher will bring a different expertise and strategy for meeting this vision, but all will share the ultimate goal. This sharing of a common purpose also helps to unite a staff of individuals.

Effective teams also establish clearly defined roles. As a team, each person's responsibilities are delineated. The team determines what each person will do and will not do. Often, role release is necessary for effective teams; responsibilities that were once part of one staff member's job description become the role of another team member. As a team, role clarification is established for the principal, classroom teacher, special education teacher, teacher aide, and other support staff members. By separating the role from the person, objective responsibilities and roles can be established for each team member.

Predetermined procedures for team operations can also help to avoid disruptions. Structured times for meetings, as well as established procedures for note taking and decision distribution, can ensure that all team members are actively involved. Establishing guidelines for conflict resolution before conflict occurs can also alleviate many future problems.

Conflict is inevitable whenever people need to reach agreements on a variety of topics. Although conflict carries a negative connotation, conflict actually motivates improvement. When different viewpoints are brought to team discussion in an atmosphere of trust and collaboration, creativity results. Objections and criticism should be heard not as attacks but as a concern to be resolved, thereby making the proposal stronger. This process can only occur in a climate where differences can be expressed without fear or resentment, which requires tolerance and a willingness to experiment and take risks. Acceptance of differing viewpoints *must* be established. Table 10.7 offers readers an informal inventory to determine their personal method of dealing with conflict. After responding either "true" or "false" to each of the statements, participants are able to complete table 10.8, which analyzes the results. Team members who had the highest totals in either "Passive" or "Passive/Aggressive" probably are not dealing with their feelings of conflict in an open manner. These

**Table 10.7. How Do You Deal with Conflict?**

| Answer each question True or False | T/F |
| --- | --- |
| 1. If you don't agree with me, you don't respect me. | |
| 2. When others disagree with me, I consider their perspective. | |
| 3. I have discovered that most people who disagree with me are incompetent. | |
| 4. I try to avoid individuals who argue with me. | |
| 5. When I disagree with others, I discuss my point of view while maintaining their dignity and respect. | |
| 6. When I am discussing my point of view and others disagree, I become surer I am correct and argue more strongly. | |
| 7. If I know that people don't agree with my viewpoints, I keep my ideas to myself. | |
| 8. Reflective listening helps others know I am really listening to their ideas. | |
| 9. Discussions are win/lose events. | |
| 10. Discussions are lose/lose events. | |
| 11. Discussions are win/win events. | |
| 12. Being belligerent helps others to see my point of view. | |
| 13. I will not get into arguments with anyone. | |
| 14. I need to convince people that I am right and they are wrong. | |

participants are keeping their anger to themselves and not sharing their emotions. Members who highest score was in the "Aggressive" area are demonstrating their anger in a belligerent or argumentative manner. Other team members are often intimidated by these members and become even more passive in their responses for fear of retaliation. Participants should strive to become assertive team members, voicing their opinions in a kind and constructive way without hiding their feelings or intimidating others.

The facilitator should encourage a brief period of personal reflection, not to be shared with teammates. Each person should decide whether he is dealing with conflict in an assertive method, voicing one's opinion without negatively affecting other team members. It

**Table 10.8.   How Do You Deal with Conflict?**

Circle the Xs if you answered the question "True."
Add the totals at the bottom of each column.

| Question | Passive | Passive/Aggressive | Assertive | Aggressive |
|---|---|---|---|---|
| 1 | X | X | | |
| 2 | | | X | |
| 3 | | | | X |
| 4 | X | X | | |
| 5 | | | X | |
| 6 | | | | X |
| 7 | X | X | | |
| 8 | | | X | |
| 9 | | | | X |
| 10 | X | X | | |
| 11 | | | X | |
| 12 | | | | X |
| 13 | X | X | | |
| 14 | | | | X |
| TOTALS | | | | |

should be stressed that while aggression is certainly not a preferred method of handling stress, passive and passive-aggressive methods are just as detrimental to the team. Team members who do not share their opinions regarding matters that affect all team members are not sharing in the responsibility of decision making. Additionally, these passive and passive-aggressive team members may express their frustration regarding decisions at a later time, well after decisions have been made. They may feel anger or frustration that the decision was not to their liking, even though they did not share their opinions. All team members should be encouraged to move toward the assertive method of handling conflict.

Several methods have been proved effective in resolving conflict. Fisher and Ury (1981) believe the win-win method of negotiations is valuable. In this method, team members separate the people from the problem, letting go of egos. The focus is on interests, not positions. Members find compatible interests and define conflicting interests. Options for mutual gain are determined through brainstorming without judgment. This requires flexibility by all members and a release from the common "their problem is not my concern" mentality. BATNA is the "Best Alternative to a Negotiated Agreement." It is the standard against which all proposals are measured. Each team member decides her own "bottom line," what is required from options, and what is negotiable. Each member's interests are explored and an acceptable alternative is developed.

Compromising involves offering a concession to one's own position. Utilizing the compromising method requires a willingness to move on rather than to defend one's own viewpoint. It is necessary to discipline oneself in order to maintain team cohesion. At times, especially involving relatively unimportant decisions, this method is quick and effective.

When utilizing the consensus method of decision making, decisions are made by consensus if all members in a group agree on the decision. The group must find a solution that every member can accept, even though some members may not be convinced that it is the best solution. What is "right" is the best collective judgment of the group as a whole. Problems are solved when individual group members accept responsibility for both listening and contributing; everyone is included in the decision-making process. Each member is responsible for monitoring the decision-making process and for initiating discussion about the process if it becomes ineffective. Decisions should be supported only if a team member agrees at least in part. The majority does not rule in the consensus method; instead, a decision is made that meets the needs of each member at least in part. Accommodation of personal interests, trust, respect, cooperation, and unity of purpose are required so that consensus can be reached. It is imperative that members accept and support the decision after consensus is determined. Members may not remain quiet during discussion only to refute the decision after it is made.

Effective teams blossom in a climate of community. This environment displays kindness towards members and hospitality toward strangers. Members generously give of their time and their ability to listen to colleagues. Compassion and forgiveness are demonstrated. A positive culture in a school can be shaped through celebrations, empowerment, commitment, flexibility, and tolerance. It is imperative that these qualities be modeled from the top down, beginning with administrators.

In addition, successful teams have a common belief system, with shared responsibilities and praise. Parity between members is demonstrated.

Members creatively plan new ideas while measuring and modifying current strategies. They agree to base conflicts on issues and not on personalities while working to improve interpersonal skills.

When synergy is experienced, when team members come to school excited about the prospects of teaching, when conflicting ideas are respected and encouraged, and when each team member is accepted for what he can offer the team, students are the beneficiaries of the combined energy and enthusiasm.

# RULES

Rule #1:
    Always Remember the Purpose of Instruction

Rule #2:
    Always Begin with Success

Rule #3:
    The Classroom Teacher Is the Expert in Curriculum; the Special
    Education Teacher Is the Expert in Special Methods

Rule #4:
    Always Remember the Purpose of Assessment

Rule #5:
    Use Baby Steps

Rule #6:
    The Older the Child, the Bigger the Gap

Rule #7:
    Always Begin with the End in Mind

Rule #8:

> The More Disorganized the Child Is Internally, the More
> Structured the Learning Environment Must Be

Rule #9:

> Visual Cues Are Easier to Remove Than Verbal Cues

Rule #10:

> Develop a Relationship

# BIBLIOGRAPHY

Alley, G., and D. Deshler. 1979. *Teaching the learning disabled adolescent: Strategies and methods.* Denver, Colo.: Love.

Anderson, J. 1999. *Exploring second language reading: Issues and strategies.* Boston: Heinle and Heinle.

Aubrey, C., and P. Felkins. 1988. *Teamwork: Involving people in quality and productivity improvement.* Milwaukee, Wis.: Quality Press.

Bernard, B. 1995. Fostering resiliency in urban schools. In *Closing the achievement gap: A vision to change in beliefs and practice,* edited by B. Williams. Oak Brook, Ill.: Research for Better Schools and North Central Regional Educational Laboratory.

Bloom, B. 1956. *Taxonomy of educational objectives: The classification of educational goals, Handbook I, cognitive domain.* New York: Longman, Green.

———. 1986. *Taxonomy of educational objectives: Handbook of the cognitive domain.* New York: Longman.

Brown, G. 1990. *Reconstructing to promote learning in America's schools videoconference #9: Reconnecting students at risk to the learning process.* Oak Brook, Ill.: North Central Regional Educational Laboratory.

Canter, L., and M. Canter. 1976. *Assertive discipline.* Santa Monica, Calif.: Canter and Associates.

Canter, A., and S. Carroll. 1998. *Helping children at home and school.* Bethesda, Md.: National Association of School Psychologists.

Choate, J. 1993. Special needs of special populations. In *Successful main-streaming: Proven ways to detect and correct special needs*, edited by J. Choate. Needham Heights, Mass.: Allyn and Bacon.

Covey, S. 1990. *The seven habits of highly effective people: Powerful lessons in personal change.* New York: Simon and Schuster.

Deshler, D., and J. Shumaker. 1986. *Learning Strategies.* Denver, Colo.: Love.

Driekurs, R. 1968. *Psychology in the classroom.* New York: Harper and Row.

Ellis, E., D. Deshler, K. Lenz, J. Schumaker, and F. Clark. 1991. An instructional model for teaching learning strategies. *Focus on Exceptional Children*, no. 236: 1–24.

Epstein, J. 1984. *Single parents and the schools: The effect of marital status on parent and teacher evaluations.* Baltimore, Md.: Johns Hopkins University, Center for Social Organization of Schools.

Farner, C. 1996. Mending the broken circle. *Learning* 8: 27–29.

Fisher, R., and W. Ury. 1981. *Getting to yes: Negotiating agreement without giving in.* New York: Penguin Books.

Flaxman, E., C. Ascher, and C. Harrington. 1988. *The mentoring of disadvantaged youth.* ERIC/CUE #47.

Flick, G. 1998. *ADD/ADHD behavior-change resource kit.* West Nyack, N.Y.: Center for Applied Research in Education.

Ford, A., R. Schnorr, L. Meyer, L. Davern, J. Black, and P. Dempsey. 1989. *The Syracuse community-referenced curriculum guide for students with moderate and severe disabilities.* Baltimore, Md.: Paul Brookes.

Genesee, F. 1995. *Integrating language and content: Lessons from immersion.* Washington, D.C.: Center for Applied Linguistics.

Goleman, D. 1995. *Emotional intelligence.* New York: Bantam Books.

Gordon, I. 1978. *What does research say about the effects of parent involvement on school?* Paper presented at the annual meeting of the Association for Supervision and Curriculum Development.

Graham, S. 1997. *Effective language learning.* Clevedon, England: Multilingual Matters.

Graham, S., K. Harris, and R. Reid. 1992. Developing self-regulated learners. *Focus on Exceptional Children*, no. 246: 38–47.

Heacox, D. 1991. *Up from underachievement.* Minneapolis, Minn.: Free Spirit.

Hill, P., G. Foster, and T. Gendler. 1990. *High schools with character.* Santa Monica, Calif.: Rand.

Hixson, J. 1993. *Redefining the issues: Who's "at-risk" and why.* Revision of a paper originally presented in 1983 at "Reducing the Risks," a workshop conducted by the Midwest Regional Center for Drug-Free School and Communities.

Kameenui, E., and D. Simmons. 1999. *Toward successful inclusion of students with disabilities: The architecture of instruction.* Reston, Va.: Council for Exceptional Children.

Kaplan, S., J. Kaplan, S. Madsen, and B. Gould. 1980. *Change for children: Ideas and activities for individualizing learning.* Glenview, Ill.: Scott Foresman.

Katzenbach, J., and D. Smith. 1993. *The wisdom of teams.* Boston, Mass.: Harvard Business.

Krashen, S., and T. Terrell. 1983. *The natural approach: Language acquisition in the classroom.* Hayward, Calif.: Alemany Press.

Lenz, B., E. Ellis, and D. Scanlon. 1996. *Teaching learning strategies to adolescents and adults with learning disabilities.* Austin, Tex.: PRO-ED.

Lucas, T., and Wagner, S. 1992. The native language: A powerful tool which supports learning. *TESOL Journal,* no. 8: 6–13.

Maeroff, G. 1990. Getting to know a good middle school. *Phi Delta Kappan* (Shoreham-Wading River), no. 71: 505–11.

Meichenbaum, D. 1975. *Training steps for metacognition.* New York: Plenum.

Mohan, B. 1986. *Language and content.* Reading, Mass.: Addison Wesley.

Nagy, W. 1988. *Psychology of behavior in the classroom.* Hillsdale: Erlbaum.

National Insitutes of Health. 1993. *Learning Disabilities,* NIH Publication No. 93-3611, Washington, D.C.: U.S. Government Printing Office

Oxford, R. 1990. *Language learning strategies: What every teacher should know.* Boston: Heinle and Heinle.

Rogers, C. 1969. *Freedom to learn.* Columbus, Oh.: Charles E. Merrill.

Salomone, A. 1992. Student-teacher interactions in selected French immersion classrooms. In *Life in language immersion classrooms,* edited by E. B. Bernhardt, 97–109. Philadelphia: Multilingual Matters.

Scarcella, R., and R. Oxford. 1992. *The tapestry of language learning: The individual in the communicative classroom.* Boston: Heinle and Heinle.

Shaw, S. 1999. IDEA 97 and "slow learners." *NASP Communique* 28, no. 5: 103.

Skinner, B. 1982. *Skinner for the classroom.* Champaign, Ill.: Research Press.

Smutny, J., S. Walker, and E. Meckstroth. 1997. *Teaching young gifted children in the regular classroom: Identifying, nurturing, and challenging ages 4-9.* Minneapolis, Minn.: Free Spirit Press.

Sturomski, N. 1997. Interventions for students with learning disabilities. *NICHCY* 25: 1–21.

Swain, M. 1988. Manipulating and complementing content teaching to maximize second language learning. *TESL Canadian Journal* 6: 68–83.

Swift, M., and G. Spivack. 1975. *Alternate teaching strategies.* Champaign, Ill.: Research Press.

Tomlinson, C. 1997. *Differentiating instruction: Facilitator's guide.* Alexandria, Va.: Association for Supervision and Curriculum Development.

———. 1999. *The differentiated classroom: Responding to the needs of all learners.* Alexandria, Va.: Association for Supervision and Curriculum Development.

———. 2001. *How to differentiate instruction in mixed-ability classrooms.* 2nd ed. Alexandria, Va.: Association for Supervision and Curriculum Development.

Tomlinson, C., and S. Allan. 2000. *Leadership for differentiating schools and classrooms.* Alexandria, Va.: Association for Supervision and Curriculum Development.

Tuckman, W. 1965. *Group theory and group skills.* New York: Prentice Hall.

White, B. 1995. *Raising a happy, unspoiled child.* New York: Simon and Schuster.

Winebrenner, S. 1992. *Teaching gifted kids in the regular classroom.* Minneapolis, Minn.: Free Spirit Press.

———. 1996. *Teaching kids with learning difficulties in the regular classroom.* Minneapolis, Minn.: Free Spirit Press.

Will, M. 1986. Educating students with learning problems: A shared responsibility. *Exceptional Children* 86, no. 2: 411–15.

Wolfgang, C., and C. Glickman. 1980. Solving discipline problems: Strategies for classroom teachers. Boston: Allyn and Bacon.

# INDEX

*Numbers in italics reference pages with tables.*

**A**

assessment: alternative methods, 18, 54; English as a second language (ESL), 53, *54;* learning disabled/slow learners, *47*, 48; students with cognitive impairments, 22–27

at-risk students, 67–72; mentoring, 71–72; motivating, 69–71

attention deficit disorders, 29–35; similarities/differences (ADD/ADHD), 35

**B**

"Best Alternative to a Negotiated Agreement" (BATNA), 96–97

Bloom's Taxonomy, 7, *8, 9, 10,* 62

**C**

Canter, L. and M., 82

classroom management, 73–85; applied behavioral analysis, 78–79; *Assertive Discipline,* 82–83; contracts (sample of behavior), *84;* phases of discipline, 76; proactive vs. reactive strategies, *84;* purpose of behavior, 79–82; qualities of effective classrooms, 73–74, 77–78

cognitive impairment, 21–28

conflict, 94, *95,* 96

contracts: behavioral, 83–*84;* learning, 62, *64*

core curriculum, 14–18; unit focus, *15*

curriculum-based instruction, 10–14; unit curriculum expansion, *16, 17,* 18; yearly project plan, 18, *19,* 20

curriculum compacting, 62, *64*

**D**

differentiated instruction: levels, *13;* methods, 2, *3, 4, 64*

direct instruction, 39, *40,* 42

Driekurs, R., 79–80

**E**

*Emotional Intelligence,* 90

emotional intelligence, *91, 92, 93,* 94

English as a second language (ESL), 19, 49–58; integrated-skill model, 55; levels of acquisition, 50–*52;* segregated skills model, 53–55; teaching strategies, 51–58

essential concepts, *see* core curriculum

**F**

functional curriculum, *see* Syracuse Curriculum

**G**

gifted children, 59–65; methods of instruction to, 60; service delivery to, 61

Goldman, D., *see Emotional Intelligence*

grouping, flexible, 63, *64*

**H**

homework, 31–33, 69–70

**I**

impulsivity, *see* attention deficit disorders

individual educational plan (IEP), 2, 13, 18, 21, 25

**K**

Kameenui and Simmons, 44

**L**

learning centers, 63, *64*

learning disabilities, 37–48; auditory perception, 38; role of LD teacher, 39; visual perception, 38

learning strategies, 40–41, *42,* 43

limited English proficiency (LEP), 18

**M**

Meichenbaum, D., 42–43

metacognition, 40–42, *43, 64*

**S**

Skinner, B.F., 78

slow learner, 45–48; differences between LD and slow learner, *47–48*

Syracuse Curriculum, 22–27

**T**

teaching style, 74–75

teaming, 87–98; climate, 87–88, 97; conflict, 94, 95, 96, 97; negative teams, 90–94

tiered assignments, 62, *64*

**U**

underachievers, 44–45

**W**

Will, M., 1

# ABOUT THE AUTHOR

**Marcie Nordlund** is an elementary school principal in a Chicago suburb. Previously, she has been a special education administrator, public speaker, college instructor, and a classroom teacher in both regular and special education.